just a MOMENT

*365 anecdotes and reflections
I've shared through the years*

God bless you.
Mama Mary,
loves you!

Fr. Jerry

Fr. Jerry M. Orbos, SVD

The Society of the Divine Word (SVD) is an international congregation of priests and brothers serving in more than fifty countries all over the world. Through the Logos Publications, the SVD in the Philippines aims to foster the apostolate of the printed word in the biblical, theological, catechetical and pastoral fields in order to promote justice, peace and human development. The opinions of the author do not necessarily reflect those of the SVD community.

Bible passages were taken from The Good News Bible.

With approval from Fr. Nielo Cantilado, SVD
Provincial Superior, SVD Central Province, Philippines.

First printing 2007
Copyright 2007 Society of the Divine Word
Published by Logos Publications, Inc.
All rights reserved

Printed by Milcar Enterprises
Quezon City, Philippines

ISBN 978-971-510-198-1

Preface

We live in a fast-paced and stressful world, and most of us are weighed down by worldly cares and concerns. So before we rush into the day, and get caught up in our busy schedules, why don't we take some quiet time to be alone with God?

Never underestimate the value of a moment, especially a moment spent with God – to be one with Him in his heart. You may not realize it, but that one moment could make your day, and could make all the difference in your life.

Don't just find time; make time.
All He's asking is... *just a moment.*

Fr. Jerry

January

Mary, Mother of God

No worries

Did you know that the words "Be not afraid" occur more than 365 times in the Bible? Wow! That's a good reminder for every day of the year and more!

Someone once said, "Worry is like a rocking chair. It gives you something to do, but it gets you nowhere."

Be not afraid.
Do not worry.
God is in control.
God has a plan.

A MOMENT WITH THE LORD

Lord, as I go on, help me to be more trusting in you and less on myself. Lord, knowing that you are in control I need not worry anymore. Amen.

A MOMENT WITH THE WORD

"Blessed is anyone who trusts in Yahweh, with Yahweh to rely on."

Jeremiah 17:7

Horizons

As a young boy, I have often wondered what lay beyond the horizon. As I grew up, I discovered that beyond the horizon, there lay another horizon, and yet another horizon. I came to the realization that there is no prospect of the horizon coming to a standstill, for the horizon ever broadens, ever beckons. Soon after that, I found out that the higher I went, the farther I saw. There must be a vantage-point, a horizon where one could see farthest! Life since then has been a search and striving for the Horizon of all horizons.

A MOMENT WITH THE LORD

Lord, help me to be open to a broadening of my horizons at any point of my life. Amen.

A MOMENT WITH THE WORD

"We do not fix our gaze on what is seen but on what is unseen."

2 Corinthians 4:18

Captured

It is wrong to think that we capture a moment. On the contrary, a moment captures us. However, being captured by a moment doesn't mean stagnation, but moving on. When we encounter an insight, or experience a truth, or accept a reality, such moments are God's way of lighting up our paths, showing us the way and challenging us to move on.

A MOMENT WITH THE LORD

Lord, help me to be sensitive to your messages in the ordinary events and moments of my life. Amen.

A MOMENT WITH THE WORD

"Treasure my words in your heart; listen to my directions and you will live."

Proverbs 4:4

Candleglow moments

As we go on in life, these are the moments we find ourselves in:

The first moment is what I call the "grindsparks" i.e., the works and the functions we do day to day.

The second moment is what I call the "flashbulbs" i.e., the socializing, the entertainment, the how-do-you-do's, and the how-have-you-beens.

The third moment is the "candleglow" i.e., moments with God, moments with oneself, and with one's true friends.

The grindparks and the flashbulbs may give "blinding" brightness. So in the thick of the grindparks and the flashbulbs, do not miss the soft candleglow...

A MOMENT WITH THE LORD

Lord, help me to allow more candleglow moments for myself, for these are what really bring out the real light in me and in others and not the grindsparks or the flashbulbs. Amen.

A MOMENT WITH THE WORD

"Come, I will lead you into solitude, and there I will speak tenderly to your heart."

Hosea 2:14

The evergreens

I spent four cold winters in Seoul, Korea. Before winter comes autumn. The leaves that are green turn yellow, red, brown, and soon the trees are bare. Winter sets in, there is no green in sight.

But, there are trees that remain green – the evergreens! What a heartwarming sight to see the evergreens, standing tall and green, surviving the coldest winter.

There is yet another trait of the evergreens. When spring comes, all plants are green and flowers are abloom. During springtime the evergreens stay in the background, unnoticed and insignificant... till autumn comes, and winter sets in, and once again, the evergreens stand tall and strong, giving inspiration and warmth to the heart.

May we all become... EVERGREENS IN THE LORD!

A MOMENT WITH THE LORD

Lord, help me to be deeply rooted in You so that I can withstand all the "winters" of life. Amen.

A MOMENT WITH THE WORD

"I am the vine. You are the branches. Remain in my love."

John 15:5,9

Three wise women?

Traditionally, January 6 is the Feast of the Three Kings or the three Wise Men. We are not really sure if there were three, we are quite certain that they were men.

So be it.

But someone sent me an interesting and funny text message saying that if it had been three wise women, instead, they would have asked for directions, they would have arrived on time to help deliver the baby, they would have cleaned the stable, cooked dinner, and brought practical gifts!

A MOMENT WITH THE LORD

Lord, help me to see beyond, to see possibilities, in every situation. Amen.

A MOMENT WITH THE WORD

"Teach us how short life is, so that we may become wise."

Psalm 90:12

Brokenness

For years, I had in one corner of my room a ceramic décor with the words "You are God's work of art…Ephesians 2,10." Recently, while I was cleaning my room, it fell down and broke. Instead of throwing it away, I glued the pieces together. It is now at the center of my table to remind me that in spite of my brokenness, I am still God's work of art.

A MOMENT WITH THE LORD

Lord, thank you, that in spite of my brokenness, you continue to show me your love and compassion. Amen.

A MOMENT WITH THE WORD

"As clay in the potter's hand so are you in my hands."
Jeremiah 18:6

Call waiting

The next time you feel like God cannot use you, just remember "Noah was a drunk; Jacob was a liar; Leah was ugly; Abraham was too old; Isaac was a daydreamer; Joseph was abused; Gideon was afraid; Elijah was suicidal; John was an escapist; Job was bankrupt; Jeremiah was a crybaby; the disciples fell asleep while praying; Peter denied his Master; and...Lazarus was dead!"

Jesus calls ordinary, seemingly useless and unqualified men to become His disciples. Peter himself says it all when He tells Jesus: "Depart from me Lord, for I am a sinful man." This statement captures the reality of someone who is called. Discipleship is not so much a matter of worthiness, but the willingness to be used by God for His mission.

A MOMENT WITH THE LORD

Lord, help me not to miss Your call and not to keep the people waiting. Amen.

A MOMENT WITH THE WORD

"Look, I stand at the door and knock. If you hear my call and open the door, I will come in to you and have supper with you."

Revelations 3:20

Awesome

To be asked the question "Do you love me?" is an awesome moment. A husband may dodge it by uttering a cliché, or pass over it with humor, or give a sigh with that faraway look in his eyes. But when it is the Lord Himself who asks us the question, before His all knowing and all-loving presence, all we can utter is, "Lord, you know everything." And hopefully we can further say, "You know that I love you."

We say and profess a lot of things in this life, but in the end, what matters most is that we can tell God that we really tried to love Him.

A MOMENT WITH THE LORD

Lord, when the moment comes, let me be ready to answer you with all my heart that I tried to love you in my lifetime. Amen.

A MOMENT WITH THE WORD

"Probe me, O God, and know my heart; try me and know my thoughts."

Psalm 139:23

You're not Him

Seen posted on a refrigerator: To all our visitors, there are only two rules in this house: There is a God, and you're not Him.

Jesus reminds us that there is a God, and we His creatures are supposed to obey and follow Him. A lot of our problems and miseries happen whenever we play God, and refuse to obey and follow Him. Take a look at your life. Miserable? Empty? Maybe it is because you have forgotten the most basic truth in this life that there is a God, and you are not Him.

A MOMENT WITH THE LORD

Lord, Help me to stop playing God because You, and You alone are God. Amen.

A MOMENT WITH THE WORD

"God resists the proud, but gives grace to the humble."

James 4:6

Disturb me

I always write my column sitting down by my desk, beside an elevated altar with a statue of the Blessed Mother on top. Recently, I have been experiencing back pains which become more pronounced when I am seated. This morning, I decided to stand up and write on the altar. This not only relieved me of my back pain but also of that writers' feeling of being alone and lonely, what with Mama Mary looking over and commenting on what I write.

A MOMENT WITH THE LORD

Lord, disturb me out of my comfort zones so that you can uplift me and heal me. Amen.

A MOMENT WITH THE WORD

"Be still and know that I am God."

Psalm 4-6,11

The pearl

Do you know how a pearl is formed?

A story I often borrow for weddings is the story of the pearl. The pearl is formed by a clam, two halves joined together as one. In the life of the clam, a grain of sand could come in, causing much pain and discomfort. But the clam does not give up or split up. Instead, it envelops that painful, irritating grain of sand with much patience, love and perseverance, till after some time the very same painful, irritating grain of sand has become a precious pearl...

A MOMENT WITH THE LORD

Lord, grant me patience, endurance, perseverance. Thank you for the problems and trials – the potential pearls in my life. Amen.

A MOMENT WITH THE WORD

"Cling to the Lord, forsake him not; thus will your future be great."

Sirach 2:3

Now, not later

I would like to share with you a beautiful poem I read which sums up the urgency of loving now.

One Little Rose
I would rather have one little rose
From the garden of a friend
Than to have the choicest flowers
When my stay on earth must end…
I would rather have one pleasant word
In kindness said to me
Than flattery when my heart is still
And life has ceased to be…
I would rather have a loving smile
From friends I know are true
Than tears shed 'round my casket
When this world I'd bid adieu…
Bring me all your flowers today
Whether pink, or white, or red
I'd rather have one blossom now
Than a truckload when I'm dead.

A MOMENT WITH THE LORD

Lord, help me to love now. Help me not to postpone my loving. Amen.

A MOMENT WITH THE WORD

"Now it is high time to wake out of sleep; For now our salvation is nearer than when we first believed."

Romans 13:11

A scorpion moment

Do you sometimes feel like giving up loving? Do you feel like giving up your goodness? Please don't.

Take time to read this story. There was this Hindu who saw a scorpion floundering around in the water. He decided to save it by stretching out his finger, but the scorpion stung him. The man still tried to get the scorpion out of the water, but the scorpion stung him again.

A man nearby told him to stop saving the scorpion that kept stinging him, but the Hindu said: "It is the nature of the scorpion to sting. It is my nature to love. Why should I give up my nature to love just because it is the nature of the scorpion to sting?"

Don't give up loving.

Don't give up your goodness.

Even if people around you sting.

A MOMENT WITH THE LORD

Lord, help me to love and keep on loving in spite of hurts, and to hold on to the goodness within me. Amen.

A MOMENT WITH THE WORD

"Leave it to the Lord and wait for him; be not vexed at the successful path of the man who does malicious deeds. Give up your anger, forsake wrath; be not vexed, it will only harm you."

Psalm 37:7-8

St. Arnold Janssen

Today is the feast of St. Arnold Janssen, the founder of our congregation, the Society of the Divine Word (SVD). He is also the founder of the Sister Servants of the Holy Spirit (S.Sp.S.), and the Pink Sisters (S.Sp.S.AP)

St. Arnold Janssen experienced a lot of "prunning". A lot of people thought he was a fool to start a mission house at a time when there was religious persecution in Germany in 1875. Many of his co-workers abandoned him, but he held on to the vision and mission God spelled out for him. He was stubborn and unbending when it came to doing God's will. Here was a man who persisted and persevered, and remained in His love, no matter what.

A MOMENT WITH THE LORD

Lord, help me to remain in You and hold on to You no matter what. St. Arnold Janssen, pray for us. Amen.

A MOMENT WITH THE WORD

"Let us not grow weary while doing good, for in due season we shall reap if we do not lose heart."

Galatians 6:9

A jewel

I heard someone say that parents are like diamond cutters. If they make the right cuts at the right angles, at the right proportions, they can produce a precious jewel. If they make the wrong cuts — because of insensitivity, neglect, or recklessness—they can shatter the precious stone forever and come up with worthless pieces of glass.

Parents, are you producing precious gems, or worthless pieces of glass?

A MOMENT WITH THE LORD

Lord, help us make precious jewels out of the little ones. Amen.

A MOMENT WITH THE WORD

"But we were gentle when we were with you, like a mother taking care of her children."

I Thessalonians 2:7

On your knees

There is an interesting story about a woman who climbed the Alps with two experienced guides. As they neared the peak, she ran toward the wonderful view and was almost blown away by the wind. One of the guides caught her and pulled her down saying: "On your knees, madam! You are safe here only on your knees."

The story is a beautiful reminder for those in high places to learn to be humble and to really listen. As long as a person sees himself / herself smaller than God, then, there is no problem. As long as he or she knows how to kneel before God, he or she will not fall.

A MOMENT WITH THE LORD

Lord, teach me how to fade away and to work for your glory. Amen.

A MOMENT WITH THE WORD

"Clothe yourselves with humility in your dealings with one another."

I Peter 5:5

When summer is gone

I once saw an elderly couple holding hands as they walked slowly. Not wanting to let the occasion pass, I went up to them and told them how inspired and edified I was to see them being so sweet and tender to each other after all the years. "Well, not really. You see, at our age, if I don't hold her hands, she'll fall down," was the old man's reply.

The key here is commitment, which is the foundation of all true loving. Long after the romance has died, long after the idealism and the feelings have faded, long after summer is gone, love survives because of commitment. Maybe you are not so much "in love" now, but are you still committed?

A MOMENT WITH THE LORD

Lord, help me to go on loving, when, and especially so, when summer is gone. Amen.

A MOMENT WITH THE WORD

"There is no limit to love's forbearance, to it's trust, it's hope, it's power to endure."

I Corinthians 13:7

More than words

In a scene of the stage play and movie, "Fiddler on the Roof", the hero Teyve on one occasion keeps nagging at his wife, Golda, asking her whether she loves him or not. He keeps wanting her to say she does...but she brushes him off several times, until she turns to him and says, "Look at this man...I cook your meals, wash your clothes, milk the cows...and after all that, you want to know whether I love you? Oh, well, I suppose I do."

A MOMENT WITH THE LORD

Lord, remind me that love is more than words. Amen.

A MOMENT WITH THE WORD

"You know my heart and its ways; You know what passed my lips; it is present before you."

Jeremiah 17:16

Why me, Lord?

Allow me to share with you the song, "Why Me, Lord?" (by Kris Kristofferson), a song which has become a song of my life.

Why me, Lord
What have I ever done to deserve even one
of the pleasures I've known
Tell me, Lord, what did I ever do
that was worth loving you
for the kindness you've shown.
Lord, help me, Jesus, I've wasted it so
Help me, Jesus, I know what I am
But now that I've known that I needed you so
Help me, Jesus
My soul's in your hands.
Try me, Lord, if you think there's a way
I can try to repay, all I've taken from you
Maybe, Lord, I can show someone else what I've
been through myself on my way back to you.

A MOMENT WITH THE LORD

Lord, thank you for loving me and not giving up on me, in spite of me. Amen.

A MOMENT WITH THE WORD

"As the Father has loved me, so I have loved you. Remain in my love."

Luke 15:9

Fertile moments

In my 27 years as a priest, I have prayed over many childless couples for the gift of a child. And to date, I can count 32 couples who came back to tell me that their request has been granted. Of course, I attribute this gift to the Lord, with whom nothing is impossible, and to the Blessed Mother's most powerful intercession. The only requirement I ask is for the couple to pray the rosary every day.

However, I realized that simple and innocent realities can become quite embarrassing, such as when a woman whom I have prayed over, greeted me at a party shouting "Oh, Father Orbos, you know, because of you, I am pregnant already!" It did not help any when, realizing her carelessness, she tried to explain to the people around that what she meant was, I was the "fertility priest", *yong paring nakakabuntis!*"

A MOMENT WITH THE LORD

Lord, even the best of my work and intentions can be misunderstood. Help me to go on, anyway, and to be grateful for whatever comes my way. Amen.

A MOMENT WITH THE WORD

"In everything, give thanks!"

I Thessalonians 5:18

Climbing mountains

According to the story I heard, one day a man, feeling tired and disheartened by life's countless trials and hardships, prayed and complained to God. "Lord, why do I have so many mountains and hills to climb in life?" he asked. And God answered: "For you to have a better view, my child."

It's not easy to climb a mountain, but the climb itself is it's own reward. Don't give up. Go slowly, step by step, one day at a time. Don't rush the climb. Learn from the climb, for he who climbs learns to travel light and leaves luggage behind. So if you are on a mountain climb right now, maybe God is freeing you from unnecessary attachments and excess baggages that you don't need in life.

A MOMENT WITH THE LORD

Lord, when burdened by the mountain climb, remind me that You are with me every single step along the way and that there's a beautiful view at the top. Amen.

A MOMENT WITH THE WORD

"A man's heart plans his way; but the Lord directs his steps."

Proverbs 16:9

My dog and the three vows

My dog, Mico, has taught me about the three vows in a very simple way.

Vow of Poverty

Well, my dog has nothing literally. In fact, he is dependent solely on me, his master. He has no savings, except perhaps, a bone or two buried somewhere. He lives one day at a time.

Vow of Obedience

Mico always tries to please me, his master, and he obeys my commands joyfully (with a dog smile, even!).

Vow of Chastity

In one of our joggings together, he saw a she-dog and wanted to stop. He looked at me and the she-dog, a sure case of being "torn between two lovers," of being "caught between good-bye and I love you." I called his name. He left the she-dog and followed me, his master.

In that single moment, I understood the vow of chastity, the sacrifice of leaving all that is beautiful and dear, to follow your master!

A MOMENT WITH THE LORD

Lord, please continue to sustain me in my resolve to seek You more than earthly riches, more than my will, more than my desires. Amen.

A MOMENT WITH THE WORD

"Seek first his kingship over you, his way of holiness, and all these things will be given you besides."

Matthew 6:33

The master

The story is told about a young boy who somehow found his way to the stage and started playing "Twinkle, Twinkle Little Star". Pederewski, the great pianist sat beside him and whispered in the boy's ear, "Don't quit. Keep playing." Soon he started accompanying the little boy in the piano, and together, the little boy and the master came out with a beautiful, mesmerizing rendition of the song.

That's how it is with our Heavenly Father.

Our efforts, our works, our accomplishments are small and hardly noteworthy, but He joins us and continues to tell us "Don't quit, keep playing."

A MOMENT WITH THE LORD

Lord, continue to hold me, guide me, and encourage me not to quit, and to keep on playing for you. Amen.

A MOMENT WITH THE WORD

"Not unto us, O Lord, not unto us, but to your name give glory."

Psalm 115:1

Handkerchief and rosary

Parents, never underestimate the value of your presence, your word, and your example. For instance, I still recall how, during our childhood days, Mama would make *bilins* and instructions as she prepared us for school every morning. Last on her checklist was whether I brought along my handkerchief. Her most important *bilin* was for me not to forget my rosary.

I am now 54 years old, and to this day, I still carry a handkerchief and a rosary in my left pocket because Mama taught me to do so when I was a little boy.

A MOMENT WITH THE LORD

Lord, while I live, let me give good examples and leave behind beautiful values and memories that will be remembered. Amen.

A MOMENT WITH THE WORD

"Be a model to the believers in the way you speak and act…"

I Timothy 4:12

The cassock

Our novice master told us to make sure we also wear a smile when we wear our cassock. Also he taught us a very simple lesson —that if we missed one button, we would have to go back and button it up and do the rest all over again. Whatever needs to be corrected, must be corrected. There is no way it can be hidden. It will eventually show.

A MOMENT WITH THE LORD

Lord, I surrender to You all the mistakes and the oversight in my life and ask You to correct and heal them all. Amen.

A MOMENT WITH THE WORD

"There is nothing hidden except to be made visible, nothing is secret except to come to light."

Mark 4:22

My mission cross

The last thing I do every night before I sleep is to kiss and embrace my mission cross.

The mission cross is given to missionaries with the simple words: "Behold your companion in life...in your travels...your consolation in sorrow...your companion in sickness...in death."

My mission cross goes with me in all my travels. I have found consolation in it and I would sometimes cry embracing my mission cross when I experience trials, loneliness, sickness, deprivations and even persecutions when I am misunderstood or misjudged by people.

I can never forget an Indian priest in our seminary who was found dead in his bed one morning, holding his mission cross.

That was 1972.-

I was a novice then.

This is 2007.

I still kiss and embrace my mission cross every night before I sleep.

A MOMENT WITH THE LORD

Lord, there's nothing I can hold on to in this life but You. Thank you for always being there for me. Amen.

A MOMENT WITH THE WORD

"Fear not, I am with you, be not dismayed; I am your God. I will strengthen you, and help you, and uphold you with my right hand of justice."

Isaiah 41:10

St. Joseph Freinademetz

Every January 28, the Arnoldus Family (SVD, SSpS, Pink Sisters) founded by St. Arnold Janssen in 1875 celebrates the feast day of St. Joseph Freinademetz, the first Divine Word Missionary to China. He worked hard and sacrificed for the Chinese people. He was noted for being kind and humble, and he really immersed himself in the Chinese life.

This Tyrolese wrote: "I love China and the Chinese; in their midst I want to die and be laid to rest among them. In heaven, I still want to continue being Chinese."

A MOMENT WITH THE LORD

Lord, help me to do Your mission well, wherever you put me. Amen.

A MOMENT WITH THE WORD

"Your mercy, O Lord, is in the heavens; your faithfulness reaches to the clouds."

Psalm 36:5

A-L-T-A-R

Here's a beautiful prayer you can say after Holy Communion and during your visits to the Blessed Sacrament. With head bowed, eyes closed, and hand over your heart, pray the A-L-T-A-R prayer:

- A - Adore the Lord, who is in your heart. Accept him with joy, humility and love.
- L - Listen to the Lord, who is in your heart. What is He telling you in the silence of your heart?
- T - Thank the Lord for His goodness and love, for His forgiveness and patience, even for your challenges and problems.
- A - Ask the Lord for anything you need. Ask not for yourself but for others too.
- R - Rejoice in the Lord, whatever you are going through. Be glad, be hopeful, because Jesus is in your Heart and because he will be with you always.

A MOMENT WITH THE LORD

Lord, make my heart truly Your living altar, where I offer all that I am and all that I have.   Amen.

A MOMENT WITH THE WORD

"Let my prayer be incense before You, my uplifted hands an evening sacrifice."

Psalm 141:2

Magic moments

Tired after a long day, and exhausted from the Manila traffic, I finally made it to the hospital for a sick call on a girl who had leukemia. In one dark corner, I saw her, this little girl of six or so, all by herself lying in the big hospital bed. My heart was crying to see her all alone, her tiny slippers on the floor, a banana on her small table, a plastic cup and a *tabo*.

I introduced myself and gave her my blessing with all tenderness and love. I donned on her a scapular, took out some candies from my pocket, and did some magic tricks. Soon, she was smiling and laughing, and the place was brighter and lighter.

And so was I.
Simple moments can become beautiful moments.
Because of love.

A MOMENT WITH THE LORD

Lord, make me an instrument of peace, love, joy and hope wherever I go, whatever I do. Amen.

A MOMENT WITH THE WORD

"Whoever receives one of these little children in my name receives me."

Mark 9:37

Short lived love story

When I was a young seminarian, there was this girl who caught my eye. She was everything I wanted and dreamed of. Love, of course, wanted to be expressed, but I neither had the courage nor the opportunity. Finally, one summer day, I had the chance to meet her. With the best introduction and with my best-modulated voice, I said: "Ah, excuse me. I'm afraid we have met before." She looked at me, smiled, and said, "Ah, I'm not afraid!"

End of the story, end of summer love. On with my vocation.

A MOMENT WITH THE LORD

Lord, remind me that more than external beauty, it is the character and the heart that pleases you. Amen.

A MOMENT WITH THE WORD

"God create in me a clean heart...do not take away from me your spirit of holiness."

Psalm 51:10-11

February

Our Lady of Lourdes

Your move

For couples, families, or friends who seem to have lost the warmth and that loving feeling, maybe you can take a cue from this text message: Rearrange the letters of the phrase "WE SAT THERE", and you will come out with a beautiful word of endearment.

Clue?
The clue is that you make your move.
Don't just sit there.
Be a SWEETHEART again.

A MOMENT WITH THE LORD

Lord, help me to make the first move towards peace and reconciliation. Amen.

A MOMENT WITH THE WORD

"Love is patient; love is kind; love is not self – seeking."
Corinthians 13:4-5

Letting go

I have said so many goodbyes in my lifetime. The greatest goodbye I fear is death. Death is the big letting go, and the big letting God. In spite of the pain of losing a loved one, we must continue living and go on loving. We must accept that in the end, the people we hold dear belong to God more than to us.

An old Buddhist adage puts it beautifully: "In the end only three things matter: how fully you lived, how deeply you loved, and how well you learned to let go of things not meant for you."

A MOMENT WITH THE LORD

Lord, because of you, I can let go of those that are dearest to me and closest to my heart. Amen.

A MOMENT WITH THE WORD

"Father, into your hands I commend my spirit."
Luke 23:46

A comet moment

In 1975, a German missionary from a remote village in Abra, using a very simple telescope, discovered a comet. The comet came to be known as Boethin's Comet, after its discoverer, Father Leo Boethin, SVD, a simple missionary who gazed at God's skies every single night. He was such a simple person that he reported his discovery not by phone or telegram, but by mail. When he received his award in Manila, he had to borrow a *barong tagalog* because he did not own one.

God really blessed this simple Divine Word missionary for his diligence and perseverance. After all, how many of us can say, "my comet" like Father Leo?

A MOMENT WITH THE LORD

Lord, there are millions of stars out there, and yet You see me, You know me, and You love me. Amen.

A MOMENT WITH THE WORD

"The eyes of the Lord are on the righteous, and His eyes are open to their cry."

Psalm 34:15

BA 269 moments

British Airways Flight 269 from London to Los Angeles was delayed for takeoff for almost an hour. Finally, the captain announced that we were waiting for a seven-year-old girl who was in transit. If we did not wait for her, she would spend the night alone in the airport or in a hotel. Everybody took the delay with a good heart for the sake of a little child...

Six hours into the flight, there was a commotion. Somebody was ill and an announcement asked if there was a doctor on board. I approached the purser and told him I was a priest. He smiled and said, "Oh no. Not yet, Father. We'll let you know if we need you. Just give all of us your blessing!"

A MOMENT WITH THE LORD

Lord, whether or not people acknowledge my presence, I know that You acknowledge and appreciate the presence of each one of us. Amen.

A MOMENT WITH THE WORD

"Even if my father and mother forsake me, the Lord will take me in."

Psalm 27:10

A coffee moment

In one of our bus stops somewhere in Spain, I went to a coffee machine to get a cup of coffee. With my little knowledge of Spanish, I tried to understand the written instructions, counted the coins, took time to choose which button to press, and finally pressed one. Success! But the grinding and dripping sound of the machine was soon overwhelmed by a frantic cry from the storekeeper who was running to me, shouting, *"La tasa! La tasa!"* I had the machine all figured out, but I forgot to put a cup to receive the dripping coffee!

A MOMENT WITH THE LORD

Lord, your grace is always there for me. Help me to be ready and open to receive it. Amen.

A MOMENT WITH THE WORD

"...He gives us grace and glory. No good thing will the Lord withhold from those who do what is right."

Psalm 84:11

Ash Wednesday moment

I saw her from the corner of my eye, this lady who was all dressed up as I was distributing the ashes with the words, "Repent and believe in the gospel. From dust you came unto dust you will return." When her turn came, this heavily made-up lady said in a *pa*-cute voice, "Father little only, *ha*. My make-up, it won't go with my make up!" Wow! Here she was being reminded that she was dust, and all she could think of was her make-up!

You know what I did? I made sure she would never forget Ash Wednesday by putting a big cross across her forehead, all the way down to her nose.

A MOMENT WITH THE LORD

Lord, remind me that there are more important things in this world than I, Me and Myself. Amen.

A MOMENT WITH THE WORD

"Vanity of vanities! All things are vanity!"

Ecclesiastes 1:2

Locked out

It happened in Galilee, I stepped out of the exit door on the 6th floor of the hotel where we were staying to see the beautiful sunrise over Lake Galilee. There I was so full of peace and praise.

My morning calm turned to panic when I realized that the fire exit door had closed behind me. It had no doorknob on the outside. What was I to do now? I saw someone below and I started shouting and waving, but he just waved back. It was indeed a scary feeling to be locked out in the cold. Finally, after what seemed like hours, a hotel guest saw me and opened the door from the inside.

A MOMENT WITH THE LORD

Lord, help me not to lock You out of my life, and remind me that unless I open my heart from the inside, You cannot get in. Amen.

A MOMENT WITH THE WORD

"Listen! I stand at the door and knock; If anyone hears my voice and opens the door, I will come into his house and eat with him, and he will eat with Me."

Revelations 3:20

Keep your peace

In Canada I met Fr. Jerry Desmont, who at 70 is so full of life, goodness, simplicity and love. What a humble and joyful person! When I asked him what his secret was, he told me: "Don't let anything or anyone destroy your peace. Keep your peace. If you get angry, you lose your peace. If you worry, you lose your peace. If you get upset, you've been set up!" Behind these words is a man who has learned through the years true humility and deep trust in God.

A MOMENT WITH THE LORD

Lord, let no one or nothing destroy the peace that you put in my heart. Amen.

A MOMENT WITH THE WORD

"Peace be with you: I give you my peace. Not as the world gives peace do I give it to you."

John 14:27

Sweet moments

Husbands and wives, are you still "sweet" to each other after all these years? Do you still hold each other's hands like you used to when you were so in love? They say that newly married couples can't stop holding hands because of love. But after some years of marriage the only time they touch each other's hand is when they use it for self –defense!

Does your husband still open the car door for you like he used to? After some years, they say that when you see a man opening the car door for the woman, there are two possibilities: one, the car is new; and two, maybe the wife is new!

Stay sweet.
Stay in love.
Stay in God.

A MOMENT WITH THE LORD

Lord, let not the years and the troubles of life make us lose our sweetness and love. Amen.

A MOMENT WITH THE WORD

"Don't get tired of doing what is good. Don't get discouraged and give up for we will reap a harvest of blessing at the appropriate time."

Galatians 6:9

The act of kneeling

ry this. As soon as you wake up, kneel down! Just kneel and pray. Do not pray lying down or sitting down but on your knees. The act of kneeling, of humbling oneself before the Creator, is a beautiful gesture of thanksgiving and humility. Try it sometime, tomorrow. It does make a big difference.

Likewise, before sleeping, kneel down. Even cows and carabaos do that just before lying down.

A MOMENT WITH THE LORD

Lord, unless and until I learn to bend my knees before You, I can never really know who You are, and who I really am. Amen.

A MOMENT WITH THE WORD

"The one who humbles himself will be exalted."

Luke 14:11

Suffering, an offering

It's too bad that some people waste the wonderful opportunity to turn their "suffering" into an "offering." To turn your suffering into an offering, do the following:

- Remove "S" – **S**urrender your suffering into God.
- Remove "U" – **U**nderstand your suffering not to your own understanding but according to God's plan.
- Replace "**S**" and "**U**" with "**O**" – **O**bey God's will with trust and hope.

Your suffering has thus become your offering!

A MOMENT WITH THE LORD

Lord, let not my sufferings go to waste. Let them become my offering to You and to Your people. Amen.

A MOMENT WITH THE WORD

"For by one offering He has made perfect forever those who are being consecrated."

Hebrews 10:14

Perfect timing

On one of my morning walks, I suddenly stopped to tie my shoelaces. While I was doing that I heard a crashing sound. A few meters ahead of me, in the direction where I was going, a huge branch had fallen from a mango tree. If I had not stopped, that branch would surely have fallen on me!

A MOMENT WITH THE LORD

Lord, You are close to me, You are always with me in so many ways more than I can know or imagine. Amen.

A MOMENT WITH THE WORD

"He will command His angels concerning you and with their hands they will support you, lest you dash your foot against a stone."

Matthew 4:6

Grace and joy

I have a confession to make. I have two life companions.

Grace has been with me all these years. Grace has sustained me through my most difficult times. Grace has stayed with me and never left me, all these years.

Joy is my other life companion. Joy has given me so much consolation and comfort. Joy has encouraged me to go on in spite of my lonely moments.

I thank God for grace and joy, my two companions in life.

A MOMENT WITH THE LORD

Lord, as you have blessed me with so much grace and joy, let me be an instrument of grace and joy to others too. Amen.

A MOMENT WITH THE WORD

"In your presence the fullness of joy, at your right hand happiness forever."

Psalm 16:11

H-E-A-R-T

Take a moment to seek from your heart the answers to the following questions:

First Question: DO YOU HAVE A HEART?

Is there no more space for matters of the heart in your hard, stern, dysfunctional and cold life?

Second Question: WHAT KIND OF HEART DO YOU HAVE?

Do you have a stony heart, a wooden heart, or perhaps a plastic heart?

Third Question: WHAT ARE THE SINS IN YOUR HEART?

There is no real peace in your heart as long as you hold in it the following sins of the heart:

H –Hatred

E –Envy

A –Anger

R –Resentment

T -Timidity

A MOMENT WITH THE LORD

Lord, remove the excess baggage in my heart. Make my heart humble, simple, peaceful and loving, like Mama Mary's Immaculate Heart. Amen.

A MOMENT WITH THE WORD

"Probe me, O God, and know my heart; try me and know my thoughts."

Psalm 139:23

Sweetheart

There is a story about a little boy who told his grandfather: "Grandpa, I'm so inspired that up to now, you still call grandma 'honey' or 'sweetheart'". Upon hearing this, the grandfather whispered to the grandson: "Don't tell this to grandma, OK? You see, I've forgotten her name!"

A MOMENT WITH THE LORD

Lord, thank you for always and forever remembering my name. Amen.

A MOMENT WITH THE WORD

"Can a woman forget her own baby and not love the child she bore? Even if a mother should forget her child, I will never forget you."

Isaiah 49:15

The Pope and the limousine

The story is told about the Pope who drove the limousine himself as he ordered his driver to sit at the back of the car. The Pope stepped on the gas and before long he was stopped by the police. The arresting cop radioed his chief saying: "Sir, I think I just busted someone very important! This driver claims he is the Pope, so his passenger at the back must be God!"

As long as we know and accept our littleness and dependence on God, we will be all right. But if we play God, and begin acting like one, then we will not be at peace, and we will not bear much fruit in life. Let man be man, let God be God.

A MOMENT WITH THE LORD

Lord, remind me to accept my littleness and dependence on you. Amen

A MOMENT WITH THE WORD

"God girded me with strength and kept my way unerring."

2 Samuel 22:32

A breakfast moment

There is a story I heard about a couple who had a beautiful golden wedding anniversary celebration. The next morning, as was his habit at breakfast for the past 50 years, the husband started cutting the bread. As was his habit at breakfast for the past 50 years, he gave the end part of the bread to the wife. The wife exploded in anger, and said she was not taking that anymore, and went on a long 'sermon' about how inconsiderate her husband was all these years.

The husband, all the while quiet, finally held the wife's hand, and said: "My dear wife, did you not know that all these years, I always thought you wanted the end part of the bread? Although it was also the part I liked most, every morning I sacrificed it out of love for you..."

A MOMENT WITH THE LORD

Lord, help me to really go out of my way to express my love. Help me to love, and not count the cost... to love till it hurts. Amen.

A MOMENT WITH THE WORD

"Beloved, let us love one another for love is of God."
1 John 4:7

Word power

A husband who always came home late at night would always try to make up by greeting his wife: "How is the beautiful mother of my three wonderful children?" Somehow, he always got away with it.

One night when the husband greeted her with his usual line, the wife who was so annoyed with his style cheerfully greeted him: "And how are you, the father of one of my three children?"

Puzzled and overpowered by the statement, the husband changed from that time on and always came home early.

A MOMENT WITH THE LORD

Lord, remind me that my words can make or break people. Amen.

A MOMENT WITH THE WORD

"Lord, place a guard at my mouth, a sentry at the door of my lips."

Psalm 141:3

Korean ducks

A popular gift for Korean couples getting married is a pair of wooden Korean ducks. They symbolize fidelity and faithfulness. It is very difficult to know which is the male and the female except for one distinguishing feature: one of them has a string tied around its bill.

Guess who that is, the groom or the bride?

A MOMENT WITH THE LORD

Lord, bless my tongue, silence my tongue, use my tongue for your glory and for others' nourishment. Amen.

A MOMENT WITH THE WORD

"Thoughtless words cause wounds as deeply as any sword, but wisely spoken words can heal."

Proverbs 12:18

Within one year

"Remember me, Father Orbos?" asked a woman over the phone.

The woman was calling from California, U.S.A. and helped me recall that she is a Philippine Airlines flight attendant whom I met on a flight to San Francisco last September 5, 2001. She is 36 years old, has been married for eight years, but childless. I prayed over her for the gift of a child. After I prayed over her, I remembered saying that within one year, she will conceive and have a baby.

According to her, nothing happened in the next few months. She almost gave up begging to Mama Mary, but she held on to her faith.

And now, she was calling to tell me the good news that she was found positive in her last pregnancy test, one year after I told her that she was going to conceive!

A MOMENT WITH THE LORD

Lord, with you, nothing is impossible! Amen.

A MOMENT WITH THE WORD

"Thanks be to God for His indescribable gift!"
2 Corinthians 9:15

Goodbye moments

I have said so many goodbyes in my lifetime. These lines have helped make these goodbyes meaningful and bearable:

"Don't be dismayed at goodbyes. A farewell is necessary before we can meet again. And meeting again, after moments or lifetimes is certain for those who are friends."

(Richard Bach)

"It is only bodies that are separated, but minds and hearts remain united, especially in Him, for whom the sacrifice is made of leaving all that is dearest."

(Anonymous)

"He has gone out of our sight in order that we may return to our hearts, and there find Him."

(St. Augustine)

"You're not just a memory...you're a presence that continues to burn in my heart." (Anonymous)

A MOMENT WITH THE LORD

Lord, make my every goodbye a good bye, not a bad bye. Amen.

A MOMENT WITH THE WORD

"You feel sorrowful now, but I will see you again, and your hearts will rejoice."

John 16:22

A mother's gratitude

Mama had her cataract operation last May 2006. I remember how worried we all were, she, being 85 years old and frail.

One morning, when we all gathered around her hospital bed, she opened her eyes, looked intently at us, her children, and said, " *Mga gwapo at magaganda pala kayo!*" (I didn't realize how good looking you all are!)

It was her humble way of saying that she was alright, and that she was grateful for our love.

A MOMENT WITH THE LORD

Lord, thank you for giving me the chance to love and serve my parents. Amen.

A MOMENT WITH THE WORD

"Be thankful in all circumstances. This is what God wants from you in your life in union with Christ Jesus."

I Thessalonians 5:18

Let go...

Julius... Katrina... Elaine... Marie Kei... Mico...
These are names of children of very dear friends. They were too young to have gone back to the Creator, leaving their parents with much grief and emptiness.

Allow me to share a story which I have shared with the dear parents and which somehow made them accept and understand the pain...

Once there was a father who was beyond consolation. He grieved deeply the loss of his child. One night, in his dream, he saw little angels with lighted candles. One of the little angels looked very sad. It was his child!

"Why, child, why are you sad?" he asked.

The little angel replied, "Daddy, the Lord always lights up our candles, but every time you grieve, every time you question, every time you cry and do not let go, the light in my candle is extinguished..."

A MOMENT WITH THE LORD

Lord, there are many things that I do not understand... help me to just hold on to You and Your promises no matter what. Amen.

A MOMENT WITH THE WORD

"Let the little children come to me and do not hinder them. It is to the just such as these that the kingdom of God belongs."

Mark 10:14

Five balls

There are five balls we juggle in life –

FAMILY

FRIENDS

HEALTH

WORK

SPIRITUAL LIFE

Remember, of these five, only work is made of rubber. The rest are made of glass. Don't drop any of them. They are fragile. Handle with care.

A MOMENT WITH THE LORD

Lord, as there are a lot of important things in this life, please remind me of what is really important. Amen.

A MOMENT WITH THE WORD

"What gain, is for anyone to win the whole world and forfeit his life."

Mark 8:36

Five questions

Please take some moment just to allow yourself to be asked these five questions:

- Just what are you really doing?
- How much do you own?
- How is your love life?
- Are you happy or gay?
- Whom are you fooling?

These are very "threatening" questions – questions we would rather not ask nor be asked by others. But, we must raise them anyway, or perhaps even deepen them by raising these sub-questions:

- WHY are you doing what you're doing?
- HOW MUCH do you share?
- Is there ENOUGH LOVE in your life?
- Is there JOY in your ministry/work?
- What KEEPS YOU GOING, anyway?

A MOMENT WITH THE LORD

Lord, as I go on in life, help me to go back to the basics always and not be afraid to raise questions. Amen.

A MOMENT WITH THE WORD

"Your hands have made me and fashioned me; give me discernment that I may learn your commands."

Psalm 119: 73

Too much talk

I read somewhere that the average person speaks 30,000 words a day! (Some, maybe more!) There is always the temptation to talk too much, to keep rewinding and to keep right on talking.

My suggestion is this: If only you cut down 50 percent of what you usually (and often unnecessarily) say, you'll have more peace, and the people around you will have more peace.

Try it. Cut down 50%!

A MOMENT WITH THE LORD

Lord, I have nothing more to say. Amen.

A MOMENT WITH THE WORD

"A guard on the mouth makes life secure; whoever talks too much is lost."

Proverbs 13:3

Take it easy

A story is told about a tourist who chanced upon a fisherman strolling by the sea. Asked what he was doing, the fisherman said he was just relaxing and taking it easy. Not wanting to let the occasion pass without teaching him a lesson, the tourist went on to admonish the fisherman to work hard so that he could have more money.

"What for?" the fisherman asked. "If you have more money, then you can relax and take it easy," the tourist responded.

"Well, that's what I'm doing now, relaxing and taking it easy," replied the fisherman.

A MOMENT WITH THE LORD

Lord, help me not to complicate my life unnecessarily. Amen.

A MOMENT WITH THE WORD

"Look at the birds of the air; they do not sow, they do not harvest and do not store food in barns; and yet your heavenly Father feeds them."

Matthew 6:26

Are you full?

Fr. Jess Briones, SVD, related to me a story about a preacher who put rocks in a glass container and asked the congregation if it was already full. When the congregation did not answer, he put in some pebbles. Next, he poured in the sand. Finally, he put in water and declared that the container was now really full. He went on to say that if the process was reversed, that is, if the water was put in first, then the container would be already right away full.

Lesson? Don't fill up your life with worthless things that will never make you full. You can have all the money, power, positions, pleasures, but if you don't have God, the Living Water in your life, you are still not complete and you are never full.

A MOMENT WITH THE LORD

Lord, help me not to forget what is really important and what really matters, You, the Living Water. Amen.

A MOMENT WITH THE WORD

"Set your heart first on the kingdom and justice of God and all these things will also be given to you."

Matthew 6:33

'Hello Jerry'

I am a very busy person, but I call my Mama everyday. What's three minutes or five minutes spent for someone who never counted the hours for me when I was a child? It's the least I can do to say thanks for all her love and care, and to let her know I really appreciate her, especially now that she is old.

Usually, it is the same questions and reminders over and over again: "Hello Jerry. How are you? Your medicine? Are you eating well? Don't work too hard. Get enough sleep." To all these, I just smile and keep saying "Yes, Ma!" enjoying the presence, the love, the concern of this woman I call Mama.

No big deal. Call your Mama now.

A MOMENT WITH THE LORD

Lord, help me never to take for granted the people you have given me. Amen.

A MOMENT WITH THE WORD

"Honor your father and mother."

Exodus 20:12

March

**Our Lady of
the Annunciation**

Because of You

When I find myself sinking in work and pressures during the day, I often find myself reaching out to God by looking up and saying, "Boy, oh Boy!" "Boy" for me is "Because Of You." Try it, sing it.

When you get so engrossed in your daily work and concerns, look up and say, "Because of you, Lord". Then you realize that the reason for all that you are doing is He, and you get to see the big picture again. Suddenly, feelings of self importance and overly concerns disappear and one is lifted up again from the clutches of personal agenda, time-tables, and what-have-you's.

"Because Of You." Yes. Sing it. Pray it. It works!

A MOMENT WITH THE LORD

Lord, change my song to "Because of You" from "Because of Me", and set me free. Amen.

A MOMENT WITH THE WORD

"Whoever makes himself great will be humbled and whoever humbles himself will be made great."

Matthew 23:12

Blessed are you

An e-mail message entitled "A Thanksgiving Thought" reminds us to count our blessings.

Consider this: If you have food, clothes, and a home, you are richer than 75% of this world; if you have some money in the bank, you are among the top 8% of the world's wealthy; if you woke up healthy this morning, you are more blessed than one million who will not survive this week; If you have experienced peace and freedom, you are ahead of 500 million people in the world; If you can read this message, you are more blessed than over two billion people who cannot read at all.

So, blessed are you!

A MOMENT WITH THE LORD

Lord, thank you for my blessings. Help me to share my blessings. Help me to be a blessing and a source of blessings for others too. Amen.

A MOMENT WITH THE WORD

"It is good to give thanks to the Lord and to sing praises to your name, O most high."

Psalm 92:1

Simple questions

Children ask the simplest and deepest questions...
Why is the moon following us?
Where does the balloon go?
Why do we work?
Why are you quarreling?
Why does he not lend me his toy?
Why are we always in a hurry?
Why do we eat in the car?
Do we have money?
Why did they nail Him to the cross?
Was Jesus a good boy?
Is Christmas near?
Why are you crying?
Where are you going?
Where did you come from?

A MOMENT WITH THE LORD

Lord, give me the grace and the wisdom to really listen to a child, so that I will be reminded of what is really important. Amen.

A MOMENT WITH THE WORD

"Whoever welcomes this child in my name, welcomes Me; and whoever welcomes Me, also welcomes the one who sent Me. For the one who is least among you all is the greatest."

Luke 9:48

Are you listening?

There is an interesting anecdote about a famous surgeon who was asked if he was worried about that point in time when his hands would no longer be steady. His response was that his greatest fear was reaching a time when he could no longer feel his patients' pain.

May we never be callous and insensitive to our people's pain and cries around us.

A MOMENT WITH THE LORD

Lord, help me to be sensitive to other people's pain. Amen.

A MOMENT WITH THE WORD

"When the just cry out, the Lord hears them, and from all their distress he rescues them."

Psalm 34:18

Temptation moments

Somebody once told me that he has no temptations.

Why? Because, as soon as temptation comes, he gives in right away!

Mama told us when we were children that whenever a temptation is in progress, the devil whispers evil on the left ear, while our guardian angel whispers goodness on the right ear. According to Mama, if we succumb to temptation, our guardian angel is filled with sadness and cries while the devil rejoices. The best way to deal with temptation is to pray, to be strong, and not give an inch.

JUST SAY NO. Period.

A MOMENT WITH THE LORD

Lord, help me not to be careless with temptations and help me not to lead myself into temptation. Amen.

A MOMENT WITH THE WORD

"Stay awake and pray not to be put to the test."

Mark 14:38

Surprise!

The story is told about an 85-year-old widow who went on a blind date with a 90-year-old man. When she returned, she was upset. "What happened, mother?" asked her daughter. "I had to slap his face three times." "You mean he got fresh?" "No," she answered, "I thought he was dead!"

A MOMENT WITH THE LORD

Lord, remind me that there will always be surprises at any point in my life. Amen.

A MOMENT WITH THE WORD

"You, Lord, are all I have, and you gave me all I need; my future is in your hands."

Psalm 16:5

A happy error

He was a 44 - year-old successful man who was living life on the fast lane. He had financial difficulties and his family needed money. To end his troubles, he contemplated suicide so that his family could collect insurance and be out of misery.

One of the last things he did was to order a book on astronomy entitled, "Night Watch," which he had promised to give his father living in the Philippines. A few days later, a box arrived at his house, and when he opened it, he got the biggest shock of his life. Inside the box was a different book, "Night Falls Fast... A Book On Suicide"!

Right there and then, he knew that God was speaking to his heart. It was a moment that changed his life.

A MOMENT WITH THE LORD

I surrender to your Master Plan all the plans in my life. Amen.

A MOMENT WITH THE WORD

"We know that God makes all things work together for the good of those who love God and are called according to His decree."

Romans 8:29

Canned heart

A canned heart is a closed heart where no one goes in, and no love goes out. It doesn't get hurt. It is a well preserved heart with lots of preservatives! Inside a canned heart, there are no disturbances, no crises, no life, and no love.

How do you know if you have a canned heart?

You shut out God from your heart; You hold back your heart – your love for others; You are filled with hatred, guilt, hurts, pride and other filth.

What you need is a can opener, *abre lata*, to open your heart. God is the *abre lata* of all hearts. Allow him to open your hearts.

A MOMENT WITH THE LORD

Lord, open my canned heart, and give me instead a heart full of love. Amen.

A MOMENT WITH THE WORD

"Create in me, O God, a pure heart."

Psalm 51:12

Barcelona airport moment

What is the worst thing that can happen to a traveler? Losing one's passport, ticket, money and other valuables.

This happened to me at Barcelona Airport last April 16, 2002, during a pilgrimage tour. The thief must have seen me alight from the bus and leave my bag in a cart while I went to get carts for the other pilgrims. While we were scurrying with our carts, the thief struck without warning, and in an 'unguarded moment', my bag was gone, along with my cash collection for missionaries, and my mission cross which I treasured a lot.

I had no other papers or credentials to show in a foreign land. But I had friends, my fellow pilgrims who supported me and prayed with me throughout the whole ordeal. The experience of loss was painful, but the experience of unity and support was heartwarming and edifying.

A MOMENT WITH THE LORD

Lord, even if I am full of cares for others, help me not to be careless. Amen.

A MOMENT WITH THE WORD

"If you remain indifferent in time of adversity, your strength will depart from you."

Proverbs 24:10

Scary moment

We were negotiating a long tunnel somewhere in Italy when suddenly, the bus slowed down and seemed to lose power. I could see lights blinking all over the instrumentation panel and noticed the worried look of our driver and guide. With cars travelling over 100 kph, anything could happen if our bus stopped. I got the microphone, and I started leading my fellow pilgrims in prayer especially to the Holy Spirit and to the Guardian Angels. After some moments that seemed like eternity, the bus lurched forward and regained power to the amazement of our driver and guide who exclaimed, "I don't know what it is, but it seems to me that your prayers are working, Father!"

"All the time," I said, pointing to heaven with a smile.

A MOMENT WITH THE LORD

Angel of God, my Guardian dear, to whom His love commits me here. Ever this day be at my side, to light and guard, to rule and guide. Amen.

A MOMENT WITH THE WORD

"He has given His angels orders about you, to guard you wherever you go."

Psalm 91:11

A nervous tourist

The story is told about Dan Torres from Bicol who was so afraid and nervous because of his illegal immigration status in the United States. When told by the guy at a gas station to "pay first," he thought the guy was asking for his papers. When asked if he had a Master card or Visa credit card, he got nervous all the more because he thought that the guy was asking for his visa. When asked whether he was a tourist, he got scared thinking that the guy knew his name was Torres. And when the guy told him to "be cool", he fainted in fear because he thought the guy even knew that he was from Bicol!

A MOMENT WITH THE LORD

Lord, I need not fear because you are near. Amen.

A MOMENT WITH THE WORD

"Fear not, I am with you, be not dismayed, I am your God."

Isaiah 41:10

Look up

Have you ever seen a person so engrossed with text messaging in his cellphone? That is the exact picture of many of us, so busy with our own world, totally unmindful of people around us, and insensitive to the stirrings of the divine within and above us. Likewise, a person so caught up with this "small screen" must learn to look up so that he can see the "big picture."

A MOMENT WITH THE LORD

Lord, let my gaze always be fixed on you and not on my little world as I travel on. Amen.

A MOMENT WITH THE WORD

"Set your mind on things above, not on things on the earth."

Colossians 3:2

Normal

In a mental asylum, an insistent reporter asked the doctor in charge how they would know if a person is "normal" already. The doctor said: "We do the bathtub test. That is, we fill the bathtub with water and give the patient a spoon, a cup, and a bucket, and ask him to empty the bathtub." "Aha! A 'normal' person would of course use the bucket, right?" asked the reporter. "No, a 'normal' person would just pull the drain plug! Would you want a room or a ward?" was the doctor's reply.

A MOMENT WITH THE LORD

Lord, help me not to be judgmental. Amen.

A MOMENT WITH THE WORD

"My son, hold on to sound judgment and discretion and do not let them out of your sight."

Proverbs 3:21

Remorse

I heard a sad story about a father who, while cleaning his brand-new car, heard a scratching sound, and saw his 8-year-old son writing something on the car door. In a fit of anger, he hit the hand of his son so hard unknowingly with a wrench that the boy had to be brought to the hospital.

When he came home, he looked at the car door and on it were the words written: "I love you Daddy..."

A MOMENT WITH THE LORD

Lord, help me to love people and not things, in this life. Amen.

A MOMENT WITH THE WORD

"As the Father has loved me, so I have loved you. Remain in my love."

Luke 15:9

B-A-G-E-T-S-S-S

To be always fresh and vibrant in our spiritual life, we must always be BAGETSSS:

- B - *Balik Panginoon* (Return to God). Whenever you fall (and we all fall), make a good confession.
- A - *Alis Galit* (Free Yourself from Anger). Do not carry useless junk and heavy metals in your heart. Forgive!
- G - *Gawa Mabuti* (Do Good Deeds.) While you live, help share, give and do good.
- E - Express your Love. Take time to relate with your God. Let people especially your loved ones, know and feel your love for them.
- T - *Tanggal Bisyo* (Get Rid of Your Vices). Take "the road less traveled," the road of clean living, sanctity, and holiness.
- S - *Sakripisyo* (Sacrifice). Take up the spirit of penance in your life.
- S - Smile. Do everything with joy.
- S - Secret. Do everything with love that seeks not recognition or vain glory.

A MOMENT WITH THE LORD

Lord, help me to be always BAGETSSS, fresh and vibrant with You and for You. Amen.

A MOMENT WITH THE WORD

"Let your heart be glad in the days of your youth."
Ecclesiastes 11:9

The stupid donkey... and Jerry

Remember the story about the donkey who started feeling great and important when many people lined up waving palms in the midst of shouts of HOSANNA? It was not the donkey, of course, but Jesus, whom it was carrying on its back, that the people were acclaiming. This is the legend of the stupid donkey on the first Palm Sunday.

Well, I had a similar experience. When I boarded an airconditioned bus from Urdaneta, Pangasinan to Baguio, imagine my surprise when I saw all the people straining their necks looking at me as I walked down the aisle. I must have even bowed or smiled at them, only to find out that I was actually blocking the TV monitor behind me! Thus is the reality of stupid Jerry, and many others who always think of themselves, and not the Christ they carry!

A MOMENT WITH THE LORD

Lord, remind me that when I become too big, people do not get to see You. Amen.

A MOMENT WITH THE WORD

"Whoever exalts himself shall be humbled, but whoever humbles himself shall be exalted."

Matthew 23:12

Three R's

Don't forget the three R's in life!

RELAX...

Many of us are overworked and overstressed. Take a break. Take a walk. Take a vacation, even just minute vacations to rest your body and your mind, and just be. Experience the restoring power of rest and sleep.

REFLECT...

"Fine tune" with yourself, with God, and with the world. How are you really doing? What have you done in your life? What do you still want to accomplish? How is your family? Is God in your life?

RENEW...

Take time to renew and recharge. Renew your contact with God. Renew your family ties, your friendships, and your mission for people and for this world. Touch base with your own very self.

A MOMENT WITH THE LORD

Lord, remind me to relax, reflect, and renew as I go on in life. Amen.

A MOMENT WITH THE WORD

"Whatever you do, do all for the Glory of God."

I Corinthians 10:31

Landslide moment

There was this big landslide which blocked the Patapat Road connecting Ilocos Norte and Cagayan and resulted to a long line of buses and other vehicles stranded on both sides of the road. There was nothing we could do but wait and hope.

Finally, after eight hours of waiting, a bulldozer arrived, and in no time at all, cleared the landslide. The road was opened and made passable again.

The meaning of the Paschal Mystery – Christ's Passion, Death and Resurrection – became so real to me that rainy day in 1979. I understood the meaning of Christ's role in opening the gates of heaven for us.

By the way, the name of the place where the landslide occured was...Kalbaryo!

A MOMENT WITH THE LORD

Lord, I need to break through the walls and landslides that block my way to Heaven. And Lord, help me not to block others' way to Heaven. Amen.

A MOMENT WITH THE WORD

"I am the way, the truth and the life."

John 14:6

Afraid to love again

It was several years since her teenage son had died in an accident, but she continued to grieve. And grieve she did to the point that she became cold to her other son. One day, this son could not take it anymore and asked her why she ignored him. She broke down before him, embraced him, and asked for his forgiveness. She finally told him that she loved him so much. She confessed that she was holding back her love because she was afraid, afraid to love much again, and get hurt much again.

A MOMENT WITH THE LORD

Lord, help me to love again and again in spite of hurts and pain. Amen.

A MOMENT WITH THE WORD

"Be not afraid I am with you always."

Matthew 28:5,20

The teardrop

The story is told that one day, the angels from heaven swooped down to earth in search of the best gift for the Father in heaven. One by one they came back and presented to God the best gifts they found. The Father was pleased, but His joy was so apparent and complete when a little angel came up to Him, opened his hands and showed the Father a teardrop from a person he saw praying and crying in a dark chapel, burdened by so much trials yet still hopeful, still strong, still holding on.

According to the story, the Father stood up, embraced the little angel with the words "You have brought me the best gift of all. Those people who have problems and failures but still go on, are very close to my heart!"

A MOMENT WITH THE LORD

Lord, at times, the only prayer I can offer you are my tears, and I know that you understand. Amen.

A MOMENT WITH THE WORD

"A humble and repentant heart O, God you will not despise."

Psalm 51:17

What is your donkey?

Are you willing to give up your "donkey" because "the Lord had need of it?" Max Lucado ("And the angels are silent") reminds us that each one of us has a donkey that the Lord needs. Our time, our talents, our treasures are donkeys which the Lord asks of us for His use; but often, because of selfishness and greed, we do not listen to Him, or simply refuse His request.

All of us have a "donkey"-- something or someone who, if given back to God, could, like the donkey on that first Palm Sunday, carry Jesus on its back.

How many donkeys do you have in your life which the Lord could use? If you don't let go of them, you might end up being burdened by them.

A MOMENT WITH THE LORD

Lord, help me to let go of the donkeys and monkeys in my life. Amen.

A MOMENT WITH THE WORD

"What profit does a man show who gains the whole world and destroys himself in the process?"

Mark 8:36

Love concretized

I visited the family of Fr. Alan Bondoc, SVD, our Filipino missionary to war-torn East Timor. It was just a short visit, but it meant so much to them.

We can never imagine their anxiety over the safety and well-being of Father Alan. What touched me was when Father Alan's mother, Adelaida, said: "Seeing you and embracing you is like seeing and embracing my son, Alan."

A MOMENT WITH THE LORD

Lord, help me to concretize your love wherever I go, whatever I do. Amen.

A MOMENT WITH THE WORD

"No one has ever seen God, but if we love one another, God lives in union with us, and his love is made perfect in us."

1 John 4:12

Just for the weekend

The story is told that when Joseph of Arimathea was asked why he lent his tomb to Jesus, his reply was: "His disciples told me He was going to use it just for the weekend."

A MOMENT WITH THE LORD

Lord, let my love for you not just be for the weekend. Amen

A MOMENT WITH THE WORD

"The mountains may depart, and the hills will be shaken, but my steadfast love for you will never end."

John 54:10

SARS: Saved, Alive, Redeemed Servants

The story is told about a woman in Germany who did not believe in the Resurrection. In fact, her will was so specific that her tomb was to be made of solid slabs of granite fastened together by huge steel bars. She even instructed that on her tomb be engraved the words: "This burial place must never be touched." But, in time, a small sprout appeared in her tomb, and soon the sprout became a big tree. All the slabs of granite and steel bars could not withstand the life of the seed that has grown within. Now, over her shattered tomb stands a big tree, alive, and so full of life.

A MOMENT WITH THE LORD

Lord because of You and the Resurrection, I have been saved, I am alive and have been redeemed. Help me to become Your grateful, loving and joyful servant. Amen.

A MOMENT WITH THE WORD

"The God of all grace who called you to his eternal glory through Christ Jesus will himself restore, confirm, strengthen, and establish you."

I Peter 5:10

Counting on us

I read an interesting anecdote which said that after Jesus rose from the dead, He was met by angels in heaven who asked Him whom He had planned to leave behind on earth to continue His work. "Just a small group of men and women who love me," Jesus replied. The angels were concerned and asked Him: Is that all? What if this tiny group should fail?" Jesus said: "I have no other plans…"

Jesus is counting on us, on our love, on our commitment to Him. He believes in us. He trusts us. He needs us.

Unworthy as we are, let us not belittle His call, or should we belittle our response. In His work, no one is indispensable, but also, no one is unimportant. We are all invited. We are all invited to stay, and stay on.

A MOMENT WITH THE LORD

Lord, help me to stay with You, no matter what. Amen.

A MOMENT WITH THE WORD

"For I am certain that nothing can separate us from his love."

Romans 8:38

A confessional moment

There I was, sitting at the confessional after six months of getting familiar with the Korean language. As I listened to the first penitent, I could not really figure out what she was saying. At most, I thought, I understood 30% of what was said. It was totally different from what I learned from the language school.

While the penitent was talking, I just kept saying aloud, "Yes, yes," hoping that I will figure out something in the end. I prayed in my heart, "Lord, whatever this person is saying, you know," while invoking the *"ecclesia-supplet,"* a provision which says that the Church will provide whatever is deficient, as long as there is good will.

After what seemed to be hours, I gave the penitent absolution and penance and dismissed her. Then, she came back (Oh no, not again!) just to tell me "Father, you are the most understanding priest I have ever confessed to!"

A MOMENT WITH THE LORD

Lord, remind me that what people hear is not so much of what I say but what I am, what I do and what I stand for. May I be your witness in this world. Amen.

A MOMENT WITH THE WORD

"This makes us ambassadors for Christ..."
2 Corinthians 5:20

Me, forgive?

After the 9-11 incident, an American general was asked if there was room for forgiveness for the terrorists.

His answer was: "I believe that forgiving them is God's prerogative. Our job is to arrange their meeting with God."

A MOMENT WITH THE LORD

Lord, help me forgive, for without you, I will take the road of revenge. Amen.

A MOMENT WITH THE WORD

"Be kind and tender-hearted to one another, and forgive one another, as God has forgiven you through Christ."

Ephesians 4:32

A mother's hold

When Jesus was arrested, all the disciples fled and abandoned their Master. All except one –John. Why did John not abandon Jesus?

Actually, according to our Novice Master Fr. Alphonse Mildner, SVD, John, too wanted to run away. But the Blessed Mother held on to him, so he could not run away! Father Mildner always told us: "Stay close to the Blessed Mother and you will never abandon Jesus!"

A MOMENT WITH THE LORD

Lord, thank you for Your Mother who always holds us close to You and who always leads us to You, her Son. Amen.

A MOMENT WITH THE WORD

"Woman, there is your son."

John 19:26

True love

I thought I knew what love was all about until I heard the story of a young man working abroad in a foreign airline. He had an unfaithful wife. He said he was willing to forgive her. He was even willing to take in the baby sired by the other man, even if his relatives thought that was too much already. But during our talk, the wife still refused the offer and opted to be with the other man who was known to have other women besides. In tears, the husband pleaded for her to stay with him and their two children; still, she refused.

I thought I knew what love was all about until I met someone who was willing to love, and forgive, like God.

A MOMENT WITH THE LORD

Lord, teach me to love the way you love. Amen.

A MOMENT WITH THE WORD

"For I am certain that nothing can separate us from his love..."

Romans 8:38

Cardinal Sin

There are a lot of things we will remember about Cardinal Sin, but I personally would like to remember him as a prayerful man, and as a happy man. He sought refuge in prayer and he urged us his flock to resort to prayer, especially in the most crucial moments of our history. He had a strong trust not on his own power but on his Master's power and on the Blessed Mother. He knew that he was just an unworthy instrument, but he knew too that his Master will not abandon him, that is why he could smile, he could joke, and he could laugh through it all.

What an honor to have lived in his lifetime.

A MOMENT WITH THE LORD

Lord, thank you for the people who beautifully radiate your power and your smile. Amen.

A MOMENT WITH THE WORD

"Always be full of joy in the Lord. I say it again, rejoice."
Philippians 4:4

St. Joseph

Have you noticed that there are very few stampitas (holy pictures) of Saint Joseph and hardly any of St. Joseph with Jesus and Mary.

Do you know why?

Kasi siya ang kumukuha ng picture! (Because he is the one taking the pictures!)

A MOMENT WITH THE LORD

Lord, teach me to learn how to fade away and remain hidden as I go on loving You. Amen.

A MOMENT WITH THE WORD

"He must increase, I must decrease."

John 3:30

April

Our Lady of Sorrows

Tumor

On April 15, 1999, I had a throat operation to remove a tumor in my vocal chords. The doctors made a biopsy and thank God, it was benign. Still dazed with anesthesia (or was it a dream), I thought I heard over the phone a baritone voice: "Father Orbos, I heard they found a HUMOR in your throat. I understand they'll give you an AUTOPSY. Well, I hope it is not malignant, only BENEVOLENT. And Father Orbos, don't agree on local anesthesia. It should be IMPORTED, ok?" OK!

A MOMENT WITH THE LORD

Lord, help me to see humor and to see the silver lining in everything that happens to me. Amen.

A MOMENT WITH THE WORD

"Rejoice in the Lord always, again I say rejoice."
Philippians 4:4

Schonstatt

Going to the Shrine of Our Lady of Schonstatt, Germany, was a religious experience for me. When I entered the little chapel, I saw the beautiful picture of Mama Mary and Baby Jesus. For some moments, my gaze was fixed on the picture, and I felt the loving embrace of Mama Mary. You know why? All these years I have been carrying in my wallet a stampita, a picture of Our Lady and Jesus, without knowing its origin, and here I was, face to face with the original picture of Mama Mary and Jesus, welcoming me and smiling at me!

A MOMENT WITH THE LORD

Lord, You really know me, and You have made beautiful plans for me. Amen.

A MOMENT WITH THE WORD

"Search me O God, and know my heart."

Psalm 139:23

A child's pain

I remember the first time I succeeded in flying a kite. I had the school playground all to myself, and I remember shouting at the top of my voice looking at my kite while running so fast to keep it airborne. Then bam! I hit a post and fell down and was writhing in pain. After some moments, a man passed by. I thought he would help me, but he just stared at me, did not even stop, and walked on.

That was many, many years ago. The pain of falling down and losing a kite are all gone now, but I still feel the pain in my heart whenever I remember the cold, indifferent stare from the man who didn't stop and passed me by.

A MOMENT WITH THE LORD

Lord, remove indifference and coldness from my heart. Amen.

A MOMENT WITH THE WORD

"It happened that a priest was going along that road and saw the man, but passed by on the other side."

Luke 10:31

A father's grief

I listened to an old man sobbing unashamedly like a child, pouring out the pain in his heart. All his years of hard work and his accumulated wealth had backfired on him. His six children were not united but were envious and jealous of each other. Three of them had not spoken to one another for years.

But the source of his heaviest grief was the thought that his children loved him only because of the properties he would leave behind. How sad...

A MOMENT WITH THE LORD

Lord, let not money or inheritance be the cause of our pain and the source of disunity among us. Amen.

A MOMENT WITH THE WORD

"So that they may all be one, as you, Father, are in me and I in you, that they also may be in us."

John 17:21

Choices

"When she cancels a date it is because she has **to**; when he cancels a date, it is because he has **two**?!"

The playing field is wide open. We can choose to be truthful or deceitful; to be faithful or unfaithful; to be good or sinful.

The choices are ours.

The consequences, too, are ours.

A MOMENT WITH THE LORD

Lord, remind me that I make or unmake my life by the choices I make. Amen.

A MOMENT WITH THE WORD

"Cling to the Lord, forsake him not; thus will your future be great."

Sirach 2:3

Fr. Francis Madhu

An agent of truth was silenced by the barrel of a gun last April 1, 2007. Fr. Francis Madhu, SVD, our 31-year-old Indonesian confrere working in Kalinga, was shot by an assailant as he was preparing for his 5:30 p.m. Mass in barrio Mabungtot, Luboagan. He was such a simple, loving, affable and diligent person. In fact, he had just walked an hour to go to the barrio Mass that afternoon, only to be killed by someone who was known to have a criminal record, and who up to this writing has not yet been arrested. While we console ourselves that he died as a true missionary, prophet and martyr, we are also very sad and mad. Why? Why him? Why this culture of violence and extrajudicial killings in our beloved land? When will truth, justice reign again?

A MOMENT WITH THE LORD

Lord, guide us to uphold justice, peace and truth in our land. Amen.

A MOMENT WITH THE WORD

"You will keep in perfect peace all who trust in you, whose thoughts are fixed on you."

Isaiah 26:3

True love never dies

An elderly couple in their 70s walked into my office for counseling. The woman told me, "Father, we were sweethearts in high school but we did not end up marrying each other. Now I am a widow and he is a widower. We still love each other. Can we get married?"

"By all means!" I said. That was one instance when my prenuptial counseling did not involve asking couples to attend a marriage seminar or inquiring about parental consent!

A MOMENT WITH THE LORD

Lord, thank You for reminding me that love is all that matters, and that true love survives. Amen.

A MOMENT WITH THE WORD

"Love bears all things, believes all things, hopes all things, and endures all things. Love never fails."

I Corinthians 13:7-8

A whispering moment

A "sermon on the mount" sort of moment occurred in our Mass by the shores of Mahatao, Batanes. The sound system conked out. To remedy the situation, I used the "*bulong*" (whispering) system during the homily. I "preached" to the 500 or so people gathered for the Mass by whispering a message to two people, with the instruction that they pass it on, and tell the others to do likewise. It worked! All the people actually heard, passed on, and remembered more clearly the message whispered unto them, and by them.

Truth does not need to be loud. In fact, truth needs only to be whispered from the heart in order to be heard by another heart.

A MOMENT WITH THE LORD

Lord, help me to spread your word, whenever, wherever, however. Amen.

A MOMENT WITH THE WORD

"Go then, to all peoples and make them my disciples."
Matthew 28:19

Real sacrifice

It is an overwhelming experience to meet our Filipino overseas workers, and to listen to stories of their different personal experiences. The bottom line of their stories was that they left the Philippines not for pleasure, but to help their loved ones back home. It was a big sacrifice on their part but it was the only way for them to earn money to support their families.

It is really sad that a Filipino woman goes abroad to become a nanny to other people's children while her own children in the Philippines are growing up without a mother. Or to be a caregiver to old folks in a foreign land while his/her own parents are being neglected and abandoned back home.

Let's support our overseas Filipino workers.
Let's pray that someday, soon, no Filipino will ever have to leave home and country just to earn a decent living.

A MOMENT WITH THE LORD

Lord, bless and reward people who sacrifice so much for the sake of others. Amen.

A MOMENT WITH THE WORD

"Yes, God so loved the world that he gave his only Son that whoever believes in him may not be lost…"
John 3:16

Remedy

There is a story about a Filipino priest who went to Europe for the first time. When he was about to start the Mass, he realized that he was so short and the altar was so high, such that only his face was visible to the congregation.

How did he remedy the situation? With a loud voice he started the Mass, saying: "In the name of the Father..." making the Sign of the Cross with his right hand touching his forehead first, then his chin, then his left cheek, and finally his right cheek.

A MOMENT WITH THE LORD

Lord, remind me that there is a solution to every problem, and that there is a remedy to every difficult situation. Amen.

A MOMENT WITH THE WORD

"I know that you can do everything; nothing is impossible."

John 42:2

Praying with our fingers

I read somewhere how we can pray with our fingers. The thumb is the finger closest to our hearts, reminding us to pray for our families and loved ones. The pointing finger reminds us to pray for those who point and lead us, e.g. the Pope, the bishops and priests, parents and teachers. The middle finger is the biggest finger reminding us to pray for our leaders and those who govern us. The ring finger is the weakest finger, reminding us to pray for those who are weak, e.g. the sick, the poor, the lost, the dependents, the sinners. Finally, the small finger, which reminds us to pray for the children, and all the "little ones" in this world.

A MOMENT WITH THE LORD

Lord, help me to pray always, to pray well, and pray much. Amen.

A MOMENT WITH THE WORD

"Be steadfast in prayer and even spend the night praying…"

Colossians 4:2

The rings of marriage

Many of us already know what the three rings of marriage are. Well, for those who don't, these are : ENGAGEMENT RING, WEDDING RING, and SUFFERING!

Here are more rings of marriage!
BEARING
BORING
WANDERING
PHILANDERING
DOMINEERING
SQUANDERING
NAGGER-RING
CARING
SHARING
PERSEVERING

For all the couples out there, I advice you to concentrate on the last three rings!

A MOMENT WITH THE LORD

Lord, as I encountered the different "rings" in life and in my commitment, help me not to lose sight of You and the final GATHERING in Heaven. Amen.

A MOMENT WITH THE WORD

"I give you a new commandment: Love one another, such as my love has been for you, so must your love be for each other."

John 13:34

The sheep and the pig

Have you ever wondered why Jesus chose the sheep and not the pig in his sermons? He could have said "I am the Good Shepherd and you are my pigs..." (Ouch!)

The reason why Jesus chose the sheep and not the pig is because they have different traits and character.

First the sheep is a quiet animal. The pig on the other hand is loud and boisterous.

Second, the sheep is a humble animal. The pig is proud and arrogant and throws his weight around.

Third, the sheep tries to clean itself when dirty.

The pig on the other hand, stays and wallows in the mud.

Are you a "sheep"?

Or would you rather be a "pig"?

A MOMENT WITH THE LORD

Lord, teach me silence, humility, and true repentance. Amen.

A MOMENT WITH THE WORD

"A kindly turn of speech attracts new friends, a courteous tongue invites many a friendly response."

Ecclesiastes 6:5

Take time, make time

We take time today to remember our parents, our good shepherds who have been there for us all these years.

A text message I received says: "Let us enjoy our parents while they are still with us; while we still can see, hold, and embrace them and while they still can celebrate with us."

Let's lavish them with love because they labored hard for the things we enjoy now. Let's talk to them now, visit them now, and wait not for the time when they hear us no more, and our visits be made before their tombstones.

A MOMENT WITH THE LORD

Lord, help me to take time for those who took time and made time for me. Amen.

A MOMENT WITH THE WORD

"Honor your father and your mother that you may have a long life in the land that Yahweh has given you."

Exodus 20:12

Envy

A desperate weight watcher's prayer: "Lord, if you can't make me thin, please make my friends fat. Amen."

An envious person is never at peace. When somebody goes up, he feels bad. When somebody goes down, he feels good. An envious person is a very insecure person because his happiness depends on the situation of the people around him. Are you an envious person? Listen to these words from the "Desiderata": "If you compare yourself with others, you may become vain or bitter for, always, there will be greater and lesser persons than yourself."

A MOMENT WITH THE LORD

Lord, help me to remove envy in my heart. Amen.

A MOMENT WITH THE WORD

"You must all have the same attitude and the same feelings; love one another, and be kind and humble with one another."

Peter 3:8

To trust again

I was counseling a woman who was still hurting deeply because of her husband's infidelity in the past. She had forgiven him, she said, but she could not bring herself to trust him again.

I tried to help her "see the light" but it was difficult to make a breakthrough. Just then, I received this text message which I immediately read to her. "THE ONLY WOMAN WHO KNOWS WHERE HER HUSBAND IS AND WHAT HE IS DOING 24 HOURS A DAY IS… A WIDOW!"

That light moment did it.

She smiled. She saw the light.

A MOMENT WITH THE LORD

Lord, help me to trust again, and again, and again. Amen.

A MOMENT WITH THE WORD

"Trust in the Lord, be strong and courageous - yes, put your hope in the Lord!"

Psalm 27:14

A wise decision

I know of a couple who used to quarrel hard and long. Not anymore. You know what helped them? The rosary. They got tired of quarreling over the same things over and over again, so they made a decision that whenever they are in a quarreling situation, they'd just stop, and pray the rosary. At first the Hail Mary's and the Holy Mary's would come out loud and angry, but as they'd go on, they realize that Mama Mary is around, so they cool down. After one rosary, they are calm, and can talk nice to each other again. And when they are not talking to each other in the car or in the room, they break the silent treatment by praying the rosary.

Try it.
It works.

A MOMENT WITH THE LORD

Lord, thank you for reminding me that you are there wherever I am and whatever I'm at. Amen.

A MOMENT WITH THE WORD

"And we know that God cause everything to work together for the good of those who love him and are called by Him."

Romans 8:28

The match story

The story is told that there was once a family of matchsticks that lived miserably inside the dark matchbox.

One day, one of the matchsticks fell down when the matchbox was opened. He saw what the other members of her family were longing for – bright light. He also saw a man take out two matchsticks from the box. The first one was used by the man as a toothpick, the other for cleaning the ears! But his greatest joy was when he saw the man get another matchstick, strike it, and behold came forth the light! "My gosh," he said. "The light we have been looking and longing for, is within us! I must go back to my family and tell them the good news."

According to the story, the man saw the matchstick, picked it up from the floor and returned it to the matchbox. His message was: "The light is within us." Some believed him, some did not.

A MOMENT WITH THE LORD

Lord, help me to keep on believing in the goodness that is within me and within everybody, and to continue to live in the light. Amen.

A MOMENT WITH THE WORD

"You are the light of the world...your light must shine before man so that they may see goodness in your acts and give praise to your Heavenly Father."

Matthew 5:14-16

'Bread'

What "bread" are we feeding our children? For many households, the most available, the most convenient "bread" is that which comes from television. Here's a modern-day translation of Psalm 23: "The TV is my shepherd, I shall not want, it makes me lie down in the sofa, it leads me away from the faith, it destroys my soul. It leads me in the path of sex and violence for the sponsor's sake. Yeah, though I walk in the shadow of Christian responsibilities, there will be not interruptions, for the TV is with me. It's cable and remote control – they comfort me. It prepares a commercial before me in the presence of my worldliness; it anoints my head with humanism and consumerism. My coveting runneth over, surely laziness and ignorance shall dwell in the house and I shall be watching TV forever."

A MOMENT WITH THE LORD

Lord, guide us to feed the right kind of bread to our children. Amen.

A MOMENT WITH THE WORD

"I am the living bread which has come down from heaven; whoever eats the bread will live forever."

John 6:51

Regret

There is a poignant story about a 20-year-old girl who asked her parents for a car on her birthday. To her dismay her father handed her a Bible. But instead of receiving it, she threw it in anger, then left home never to return.

After some years, her parents died in a plane crash. She went to the funeral, and surprisingly she found the Bible she had refused to receive years back. When she opened it, she found an envelope with a car key and a message: "Happy birthday, we love you! The car is still in the garage. Dad and Mom."

A MOMENT WITH THE LORD

Lord, at the end of my life, may I have no regrets that I loved too little, too late. Amen.

A MOMENT WITH THE WORD

"My child, hold on to your wisdom and insight. Never let them get away from you."

Proverbs 3:21

The five fingers

Take a moment to look at your fingers. Have you ever wondered why the thumb is separated from the four fingers of your hand?

The story is told of five brothers and sisters. The parents entrusted to the eldest all their wealth and resources with the instruction that he take care of his brothers and sisters in their absence. But, as the story goes, the eldest appropriated all of what was left by their parents for himself and did not share with his brothers and sisters.

The selfishness of the thumb angered his brothers and sisters. The four retaliated by distancing themselves from him.

Yes, the thumb had all the wealth, but he lost his brothers and sisters.

A MOMENT WITH THE LORD

Lord, let not money, treasure and inheritance separate us from one another, and from You. Amen.

A MOMENT WITH THE WORD

"I pray that all may be one...that the world may believe that you sent me."

John 17:21

First honor

I received this letter from Joanna Francesca, an 11-year-old girl: "I am the second honor in my class. That's because Nicole cheats. She is not honest, so she is first honor. What can I do? No matter how hard I try, I'm still second. But it's okay. I know only God can make a way because every hard work has its prize and every mistake has its own consequence. I know somehow, someday I can be first honor. Please pray for me."

I wrote back: "By being honest, you are already first honor in God's eyes. Be assured that God knows how to count, and He knows who is naughty or nice. Continue to be good even if others are not!"

A MOMENT WITH THE LORD

Lord, help me to be honest even when others are not. Amen.

A MOMENT WITH THE WORD

"No one who practices deceit shall remain in my presence."

Psalm 101:7

Embraced by God

Someone texted me to say the Sign of the Cross slowly and end it with your hands across your chest when you say "Amen", and then let God embrace you.

Stay in this position and feel God's loving embrace and love. What a beautiful feeling to be embraced by God.

Try it. Try it now.

A MOMENT WITH THE LORD

Lord, thank you for your loving embrace. Thank you for your presence and grace. Amen.

A MOMENT WITH THE WORD

"Because you are precious to me and honored, I love you."

Isaiah 43:3

Flee and pray

Our novice master once advised us how to fight temptation with just two words: FLEE and PRAY!

Flee because it is better to be a coward than to be a hero when it comes to dealing with the enemy. Pray because it is the only way to be shielded from the assaults of the enemy.

Pray that when you have the courage, you will not have the opportunity, and when you have the opportunity you will not have the courage to sin.

A MOMENT WITH THE LORD

Lord, help me to flee and pray when temptation comes my way. Amen.

A MOMENT WITH THE WORD

"...God is faithful; He will not let you be tempted beyond what you can bear."

I Corinthians 10:13

Fame

I had a chance to visit the Museum of Egypt in Cairo recently, and I was amazed at seeing all the wealth and treasure of King Tuttankhammun. But museums only remind us of one thing: that we carry nothing with us when we leave this world.

For those who plan to amass more wealth or have more power, go to a museum or a cemetery sometime and be reminded how short life is, and how fleeting power, name and fame are.

A MOMENT WITH THE LORD

Lord, more than fame, help me to seek to do your will in everything. Amen.

A MOMENT WITH THE WORD

"For we fix our attention, not on things that are seen, but on things that are unseen."

2 Corinthians 4:18

The best advice

The best advice in confession came from an old (but not deaf!) priest to whom I made a general confession before my ordination. I poured out my heart and my soul, and the priest just listened. Finally, when he spoke up, he told me this: "My son, just remember, there is no sinner without a future, and there is no saint without a past..."

It was the shortest and the best advice I ever received in confession.

A MOMENT WITH THE LORD

Lord, thank you for giving me hope when I look at my sinful past, and for giving me courage when I face the uncertain future ahead of me. My only assurance is Your unconditional love and forgiveness. Amen.

A MOMENT WITH THE WORD

"...I give no thought to what lies behind but push on to what is ahead."

Philippians 3:13-14

Take it from the chopsticks

Take some moments, look at the chopsticks. Then look at your relationships. A relationship that is not blessed or held by God is bound to be fragile. It will easily fall apart. Allow God to hold you together.

As with the chopsticks, a relationship must be held neither too loose nor too tight. Just right. There is no fixed rule as to who should be below or above.

As with the chopsticks, one is not enough to serve its purpose. You have to stay together for a purpose, for a mission.

So, do not CHOP each other. STICK to each other because God has brought you together!

A MOMENT WITH THE LORD

Lord, continue to hold me and help me to hold others "just right." Use me to bring together and to bind, rather than "cut" and divide. Amen.

A MOMENT WITH THE WORD

"All of you should be like-minded, sympathetic, loving toward one another, kindly disposed, and humble. Do not return evil for evil, or insult for insult. Return a blessing instead..."

1 Peter 3:8

Indeed

Sometime ago I met a lady who attended my Holy Saturday recollection, and said she was touched by the words she had listened to that morning. When I asked her what struck or touched her most, she said she had forgotten already, but it was "all nice." However, what she did remember was seeing me kneel down before the crucifix just before my talk. She was early in the church, and she saw me walk in (in my jogging clothes), kneel down in prayer, and touch the crucifix. Those silent, unspoken moments spoke louder to her than all the words I said an hour later.

It was what I did, not so much what I said, that touched her most.

Indeed, actions speak louder than words.

A MOMENT WITH THE LORD

Lord, help me to love not only in words, but especially so, in deeds. Amen.

A MOMENT WITH THE WORD

"Be a model to the believers in the way you speak and act, in your love, your faith and purity of life."

I Timothy 4:12

Mission House

The Mission House in Bangued Abra was the place where we would unwind after coming from our difficult mission stations, and enjoy good food, drinks, entertainment and other comforts. Most of all, it was the place where we would meet and share with fellow missionaries our joys, struggles, experiences, and achievements. Our get together was highlighted by the celebration of the Eucharist.

I remember the chapel of the Mission House where as a young missionary I would kneel before the Blessed Sacrament, drenched with perspiration or drenched in the rain. All my weariness and burdens seemed to disappear as soon as I entered the chapel in the mission house.

The Mission House was the place where we could relax, reflect, recharge, and renew. We all need a "mission house." Do you have one in your life?

A MOMENT WITH THE LORD

Lord, may I never deny my need to relax, reflect, recharge and renew as I go on in life. Amen.

A MOMENT WITH THE WORD

"My house shall be a house of prayer."

Luke 19:46

One last look

The story is told about a taxi driver who went out of his way to pick up an 80-year-old woman who was leaving her house to go to an old folks' home. With a lonely heart, and with all her worldly possessions in one little suitcase, the lady asked to be brought around the city for the last time, down memory lane. After two hours, the taxi driver brought her to her new home without charging anything. She hugged him gratefully and said, "You gave an old woman a little moment of joy today. Thank you."

Our lives do not consist of great moments.

It's the little moments that we remember and affect us forever.

A MOMENT WITH THE LORD

Lord, remind us that people may not remember exactly what we did or said, but they will always remember what we made them feel. Amen.

A MOMENT WITH THE WORD

"The upright man will be remembered with blessings…"

Proverbs 10:7

May

Our Lady of Fatima

Sharing our treasure

Every time I travel and go around, I see how rich and progressive our Asian neighbors have become. I can't help but feel envious of the progress they are enjoying and wish that the Philippines, too, would shape up and get going real soon.

There was one moment though, in Shanghai, that made me realize that we are richer still despite our poverty. Our guide, an atheist, observed how happy and joyful we Filipinos are. She said it was so easy for us to be warm and accommodating. She also observed how prayerful we are.

She said it so well: "When I have problems, I just go out, drink and have fun, and somehow forget. But you Filipinos, you pray, you turn to God, and you are peaceful and happy again."

How true.

We have our faith. We have a treasure.

It is not ours to keep, but to spread. Not ours to flaunt, but to share.

A MOMENT WITH THE LORD

Lord, thank you for the gift of faith. Not mine to keep but mine to give. Amen.

A MOMENT WITH THE WORD

"...Go out to the whole world and proclaim the Good News to all creation."

Mark 16:25

Korean birthday

I spent four years in Korea as a missionary (1984-1988), and one of the first things I learned is that Koreans celebrate only two birthdays in their lifetime: their first and their sixty fifth birthday.

Why?

In Korea where infant mortality before was high, it is a big reason to celebrate a child's first birthday. And when one reaches 65 years of age, the Koreans already equate it to a full life. So, any year after 65 is considered as a "bonus" year by Koreans. (How many "bonus" years do you have now?)

Every birthday is a thanksgiving day, first of all to God who gave us life, to our parents, to our loved ones who fill our lives.

Every birthday, too, is like a kilometer sign post along the way to remind us how far we have gone down the road of life... and how near we are to our final destination!

A MOMENT WITH THE LORD

Thank you, Lord, I was born in this world. Thank you, Lord, I'm still alive. Help me to live a life that is full, beautiful and meaningful. Amen.

A MOMENT WITH THE WORD

"Truly you have formed my inmost being; you knit me in my mother's womb."

Psalm 139:13

Facing fear

God really knows where and when to "hit" us. In one of my visits to Naju, Korea, I witnessed a woman possessed by the devil. I excused myself from the hall thinking that the two more holy priests who were left behind could do the exorcism. Actually I was afraid. After some 20 minutes I decided to go back. I was passing this dark corner leading to the hall when someone stopped me and asked for confession. Guess who it was? It was the possessed woman!

Gathering all courage in Jesus's name, I heard her confession in that dimly lit corner. That night, the Lord made me confront and overcome my fears. The only assurance I had was that He was with me.

A MOMENT WITH THE LORD

Lord, help me to face and conquer my fears with you. Amen.

A MOMENT WITH THE WORD

"Fear not, for I am with you."

Isaiah 43:5

Ice cream and balloons

When we were children we saw balloons and tasted ice cream only once a year, and that was during the town fiesta. Oh, the joy of holding a balloon on one hand and dripping ice cream cone on the other. And oh, the pain of losing a balloon, and see it go up the sky, following it with tears in my eyes till it is only a dot, and no more to be mine... and then, still crying, half aware, I bite into the cone... and realize I still had the ice cream in my other hand!

A MOMENT WITH THE LORD

Lord, help me to focus not on what I have lost or what I lack, but on what I still have and what will still come. Amen.

A MOMENT WITH THE WORD

"...No dear friends I am still not all I should be, but I'm focusing all energies on this one thing: Forgetting the past and looking forward to what lies ahead..."

Philippians 3,12-14

Minus one

A story is told about a girl, born minus one ear, growing up shy and withdrawn and often hurt because of her defect. The mother always felt her pain more than anybody else.

On the girl's 18th birthday, she was brought by her mother to the hospital for an ear transplant operation which turned out to be successful. This changed her whole life. She became free and outgoing. And then she met the man of her dreams.

The night before her wedding, she embraced her mother so tight and she found out for the first time that her mother no longer had one ear!

It turned out that the ear transplanted to her was that of her mother whom she had often hurt, shouted at and taken for granted all those years...

A MOMENT WITH THE LORD

Lord, You had not only given me your ear but also your Heir. I know that too many times I have taken You for granted. Lord, I can never fathom the depth of your constant and unconditional love for me. Amen.

A MOMENT WITH THE WORD

"As a mother comforts her son, so will I comfort you..."
Isaiah 66:13

Last three words

If I had only three last words to say, what would they be?

After my throat operation in 1999, I could not talk. I could only whisper as the doctor gave me strict orders to rest my vocal chords. I began to feel how difficult it was to have no voice. I then realized that if I had only three last words to say, I would say to God and to those who have been a part of my life, the words:

THANK YOU...
I AM SORRY...
I LOVE YOU...

You who have voices now, say these words as often as you can to the important people in your life, while you still can, and while they still can hear you.

A MOMENT WITH THE LORD

Lord, have I told You lately that I love You? Have I told You that I am sorry and I thank you? Please make it easy for me to say these words, too, to the people around me. Amen.

A MOMENT WITH THE WORD

"Teach us to number our days aright, that we may gain wisdom of heart."

Psalm 90:12

A gift for Papa

I must have been nine years old then. Our town was celebrating its feast day and there were rides and games. My face glowed with much excitement when I won in one of the games.

When I was asked what prize I wanted from the displayed items, I chose the big drinking glass for Papa. Yes, for Papa! And I ran to the house calling his name, so happy to give him a gift, so happy to see him happy!

Yes, that was many, many years ago, but I still remember myself happily running home from the town plaza bringing the gift for my father...

A MOMENT WITH THE LORD

Lord, help me to live a life that is pleasing to You. May I become a source of joy and happiness to You and to my loved ones. Amen.

A MOMENT WITH THE WORD

"The One who sent me is with me. He has not deserted me since I always do what pleases him."

John 8:29

Affirmation works

When I was in Grade 4 at Sta. Catalina College, I had a religion teacher who never failed to compliment and affirm me. She would say in class, "Jerry, you are a good boy. Maybe you will become a priest someday." She kept repeating her encouraging remarks whenever I would do good in oral or written examinations.

The positive remarks of my teacher really made me feel good about myself and made me try to be better. The teacher made me believe in my goodness. She made me believe in myself.

Affirmation really works!

A MOMENT WITH THE LORD

Lord, thank you for all the people who made me believe in myself and in the goodness within me. Grant that I, too, become an instrument of Your constant love and affirmation. Amen.

A MOMENT WITH THE WORD

"Never let evil talk pass your lips; say only the good things men need to hear, things that will really help them."
Ephesians 4:29

A good name

I remember those candle-lit evenings when we would pray the family rosary, and later, share stories and beautiful moments in our humble home in Bani, Pangasinan. We had no electricity, we had not much in life. But we had time, we had each other and we had Papa and Mama who would always tell us, "We have no money and riches to leave behind, but we leave you with a good name... a good name you can use with pride and dignity."

A MOMENT WITH THE LORD

Lord, help me to treasure a good name more than riches, a peaceful life more than a popular life, a simple life more than a complicated life. Amen.

A MOMENT WITH THE WORD

"Neither in my youth, nor now that I am old, have I seen a just man forsaken nor his descendants begging bread."
Psalm 37:25

A traffic moment

There I was, caught in a long traffic jam that has not moved for an hour or so, in Concepcion, Tarlac. I got out of the car and was greeted by the occupants of the next car, a couple with a little baby. "How long have you been here?" I asked. "Father," said the husband, "when we got here, my wife was still pregnant!"

And we all broke into laughter...and somehow I thought I heard the angels laughing as well!

A MOMENT WITH THE LORD

Lord, help me to realize that it is not my position, but my disposition that really counts much in life. Amen.

A MOMENT WITH THE WORD

"A glad heart lights up the face, but by mental anguish the spirit is broken."

Proverbs 15:13

Express your love

"It isn't the thing you do dear, it's the thing you could have done, that leaves me with a bit of heartache at the setting of the sun". A beautiful reminder for us not to take for granted our mothers, and to express our love for them while there is time. Aside from expressing our appreciation and love for our mothers, the best gift we can give them is the assurance that we will be all right, and that we are living fruitful lives.

If only you listened to your mother, what would you be, where would you be, how would you be now? Find time today to go back, remember and renew your mother's wishes and dreams.

A MOMENT WITH THE LORD

Lord, help me to express my love to my mother every moment I can. Amen.

A MOMENT WITH THE WORD

"Behold your mother."

John 19:27

A sad story

At first, I thought it was not possible. Two women brought an old woman to the home for the aged of the Missionaries of Charity in Tayuman St., Tondo. They told the Sisters that they found her in the streets, abandoned, needing food and shelter.

After the woman left, the old woman cried to the Sisters. She was not, she said, someone they found in the streets. She was, the mother of the two...

A sad story.

But, it really happened.

A MOMENT WITH THE LORD

Lord, as You have never abandoned me, help me never to abandon the people You have given me, nor abandon the mission You have entrusted me. Amen.

A MOMENT WITH THE WORD

"...For God has said, 'I will never desert you, nor will I forsake you.'"

Hebrew 13:5

Waiting for Mama

Never underestimate the value of your presence.

I remember how as little children my brothers and sisters awaited with much joy and anticipation the arrival of Mama from the barrio school. After she alighted from the dusty bus, we would all run and embrace her, calling out her name. She was home, and that was all that mattered. Her presence and her smile was the magic that erased all our loneliness, insecurities, and fears.

Go home.

Someone's waiting for you.

A MOMENT WITH THE LORD

Lord, let my presence be a "good news" to other people. May people find in me a welcoming and an assuring presence. Amen.

A MOMENT WITH THE WORD

"Come to me all of you who are weary and carrying heavy burdens, and I will give you rest."

Matthew 11:28

True bread

One morning, on my way to a Sunday TV Mass, I was surprised, indeed elated, at the sight of a long line of people outside the studio. This was about 6:30 a.m. So I said a prayer of praise and gratitude to the Lord for sending so many people so early to attend the 7 a.m. Mass.

Then I learned that these people had lined up so early as the night before to take part in a noontime TV show that promised big monetary prizes! They were there not for the Bread of Heaven, but just for the bread, period.

A MOMENT WITH THE LORD

Lord, remind me of the importance of the true Bread come down from Heaven. Amen.

A MOMENT WITH THE WORD

"He gave them Bread from heaven to eat."

John 6:31

Psst-point

We Filipinos have a very unique way of calling others by making the "*psst*" sound. Try this sometime. When you are abroad, and you are not sure if the fellow ahead is a Filipino, a Malaysian, or a Thai, make the "*psst*" sound. If he turns his head, you've found a *kababayan*.

There is something else that is very unique to us Pinoys. We point with our lips. We are the only people in the world that point at people, things, and directions with our protruding lips!

Mama Mary is the lady who calls, i.e. *Manaoag (tawag)* and it is she who points to her Son Jesus. All of us too should be busy with our mission of calling others, and leading them to Jesus.

A MOMENT WITH THE LORD

Lord, may I never tire of calling others to come to you. Amen.

A MOMENT WITH THE WORD

"The things which happened to me have actually turned out for the furtherance of the Gospel."

Philippians 1:2

A Eucharistic moment

I can never forget May 16, 1991 when I experienced a "Eucharistic miracle" with the Korean victim soul and visionary Julia Kim. After communion, I smelled the scent of roses, and I saw Julia crying and trembling with her eyes closed. She opened her mouth, and I saw blood, and on her tongue was the sacred host, so red, like a newly-cut flesh! I laid my hands over her while I prayed, "Lord, if this is what it is, thank you, Lord, for allowing me to witness it, unworthy as I am. Forgive me, forgive us for the times we take you for granted. Lord you are really present in the Eucharist..."

It was a moment I can never forget. I do not claim a miracle here. It was an experience that has made me love the Mass more and more. And I encourage everyone to do the same. Remember, blessed are you who "have not seen, and yet believe." Also, Julia told me something that made me cry. She said she saw the Blessed Mother at my back, embracing the unworthy me, when I was saying the Eucharist that night of May 16, 1991.

A MOMENT WITH THE LORD

Thank you, Lord, for allowing me to experience Your real presence in the Eucharist. May I, in turn, be Your real presence in this world. Amen.

A MOMENT WITH THE WORD

"...Do this in remembrance of me..."

Luke 22:19

All in a day's work

I remember one rainy day when I had four sick calls: one in Marikina, two in Makati, and one in Quezon City. That meant hustling in the traffic, braving the rain, finding a parking space, and walking up several floors. All of these would have been fine except that on that particular day, I, myself, was under the weather, nursing a fever, and coming down with cough and colds.

It was not easy to love that day.

But then, whoever said that true love is easy?

Love well. Love much. Love on.

A MOMENT WITH THE LORD

Lord, help me to love on especially when loving doesn't come easy. Amen.

A MOMENT WITH THE WORD

"There is no greater love than this: to give one's life for one's friends…"

John 15:13

A moment with the Trinity

L et me share with you my "theophany", my religious experience with the Trinity during our perpetual vows retreat in 1979 at the SVD Retreat House in Baguio City. Deep in prayer, I was asking the Lord if he really wanted me to become a priest. Then I "saw" the Trinity, and I "heard" the Holy Spirit say: "Jerry, we know you, we love you. We had our meeting, and we have chosen you...!"

I felt both joyful and unworthy that very moment. Imagine, "*pinag-mi-mitingan pala ako ng Trinity*!" (Imagine the Trinity having a meeting about me!) I ended up saying "Lord, you alone will I love above all in my life. Keep me ever in your love. Remind me, always." And the Spirit, responded: "Yes, Jerry, there will always be something or someone there to remind you."

God has been faithfull all these years, and there have always been someone or something there to remind me of His love.

A MOMENT WITH THE LORD

Lord, You alone will I love above all in my life. Remind me, always. Amen.

A MOMENT WITH THE WORD

"Understand, then, that the Lord, your God, is God who keeps his merciful covenant..."

Deuteronomy 7:9

Pari (Priest) sighted

It was an early morning sick call. On my way down I rode the elevator with a weary-looking nurse. After we greeted each other I said in jest, "Hey, you know, I'm nurse-sighted." Her face really brightened up and so did mine when she answered back, "You know Father, I'm *pari*-sighted!"

A MOMENT WITH THE LORD

Lord, as I go about serving You and the people, help me not to lose sight of joy and humor. Amen.

A MOMENT WITH THE WORD

"In the same way you should rejoice and share your joy with Me."

Philippians 2:18

Didn't sink in

Wanting to remedy the presence of many unwashed dishes in our kitchen sink, Fr. Ed Fugoso, SVD, former Superior Delegatus at our Mission House put up this sign: "There is a story about four people named "EVERYBODY, SOMEBODY, ANYBODY and NOBODY. There was an important job to be done, and EVERYBODY was asked to do it. ANYBODY could have done it, but NOBODY did it. SOMEBODY got angry because it was EVERYBODY's job. EVERYBODY thought ANYBODY could do it, but NOBODY realized that EVERYBODY wouldn't do it. It ended up that EVERYBODY blamed SOMEBODY when NOBODY did what ANYBODY could have done!"

After one month, the situation did not quite improve, so he put up another sign: YOUR MOTHER DOES NOT WORK HERE. CLEAN UP AFTER YOURSELF! Since then, there are no longer unwashed dishes in our kitchen sink.

A MOMENT WITH THE LORD

Lord, help me to say the right thing, at the right time and not to stop saying it till they get it right. Amen.

A MOMENT WITH THE WORD

"Let us look, then, for what strengthens peace and makes us better."

Romans 14:19

Are you a cave or a wall?

How do you differentiate a cave from a wall?

A cave is open. It welcomes people to whom it provides warmth and shelter. A "cave" person, therefore, is someone who takes in and shelters people.

On the other hand, a wall obstructs and even divides. It is also closed and cold. A "wall" person is someone who shuts out people. One has to put up with a "wall."

So, what are you – a "cave" or a "wall"?

A MOMENT WITH THE LORD

Lord, while I live, let me be someone who welcomes and who assures people. Amen.

A MOMENT WITH THE WORD

"If you hear my call and open the door, I will come in to you and have supper with you."

Revelations 3:20

A father's example

I must have been about six years old then. One stormy late afternoon, I saw Papa looking out of the window, so worried because Mama has not yet come home from the barrio public school where she was teaching.

Then I saw Papa go to our family altar, light a candle and kneel down. I still remember him, so intense in prayer, head bowed down. Then, he summoned me and my brother, *Manong* Oscar. "Come Jerry, Oscar, let us pray for your Mama."

I cannot recall now how we prayed and how long we prayed; but I will never forget the memory of Papa, *Manong* Oscar and me kneeling down before the Blessed Mother, praying for Mama's safety.

A MOMENT WITH THE LORD

Lord, after I am gone, what will people remember about me? Help me to leave behind happy and beautiful memories. Amen.

A MOMENT WITH THE WORD

"Grandchildren are the crown of old men, and the glory of children is their parentage."

Proverbs 17:6

A mother's comfort

Yes, I admit, I would sometimes wish I had the comforts and the easy life of the rich and the famous.

Yes, it happens. Sometimes I even have feelings of insecurity, self-pity, especially when I see big houses or when I drive alongside flashy and expensive cars, while I sit in an eight-year-old car which I do not even own.

It is at such times when I feel the embrace and the smile of the Blessed Mother, and I start singing the song "Mother of Christ." And then I would smile again, affirming my choice for the "road less traveled," especially with the line of the song that goes, "I do not sigh for the wealth of earth, for the joys that fade and flee..."

A MOMENT WITH THE LORD

Lord, I left everything to follow You. Remind me and assure me again and again that everything is vain and empty if you are not present in my life. Amen.

A MOMENT WITH THE WORD

"Look at the birds in the sky. They do not sow nor reap, they gather nothing into barns, yet your heavenly Father feeds them."

Matthew 6:26

A police moment

I went through a yellow light and a policeman flagged me down. I tried to explain, but he just kept on berating me. He was tough and arrogant.

He demanded to see my driver's license. He looked at it and I noticed a sudden change in the tone of his voice.

"Ah... Christ the King Seminary...*pari ka ba?*" (Are you a priest?) he asked

"Yes, sir," I answered.

"Ay, sorry Father, *akala ko tao.*" (I'm sorry, Father, I thought you were a person!)

A MOMENT WITH THE LORD

Lord, remind me that I am only human, and I have feet of clay, yet You have made me a little less than an angel, and with dignity and honor You've crowned me. Amen.

A MOMENT WITH THE WORD

"For we have not a high priest who can not have compassion on our infirmities, but one tried as we are in all things, except sins."

Hebrews 4:15

Three flies!

I did not know how they got there, but there were three flies in the wine I have just consecrated at a Mass in Lipa! My first thought was to remove them with the purificator, but right there and then, the Lord challenged me with the question: "Jerry, do you love me? Do you believe this is my blood?"

I went on with the Mass, not quite knowing what to do. It was the longest Mass for me. Finally, at communion I said, "Lord, I love You, I believe this is your blood," and I drank the wine with the three flies and bowed my head in prayer.

Today, the flies must still be going around my system, but more than that, I carry in me a grateful heart for having been allowed to express my love for the Lord in a very palatable way in the Eucharist!

A MOMENT WITH THE LORD

Lord, I believe that You are really present in the Eucharist. Amen.

A MOMENT WITH THE WORD

"My brothers count it pure joy when you are involved in every sort of trial. Realize that when your faith is tested this makes for endurance."

James 1:2-3

'Ad-danto'

As a little boy, I always dreamed of having a bicycle. It was my perennial birthday and Christmas wish. Life was hard, and money was scarce when I was growing up. Papa and Mama had to work hard and they could not afford to buy me a bicycle, even a second-hand one. But I remember what Papa always told me.

"Bay-am Jerry. Agkararag ka laeng.
Agsingsingpet ka. Agadal ka nga nalaing.
Ad-danto. Ad-danto..."

(Never mind Jerry. Just pray. Be good. Study well. There will be someday, there will be...)

Papa and Mama never gave me a bicycle, but they gave me a dream, a vision.

They gave me hope.

A MOMENT WITH THE LORD

Lord, help me to keep on dreaming and believing, confident that You listen to every prayer, and that You make all things beautiful in your time. Amen.

A MOMENT WITH THE WORD

"So, may God, the source of hope, fill you with all joy and peace in believing so that through the power of the Holy Spirit you may have hope in abundance."

Romans 15:13

Are you depressed?

I was hurrying up for an early morning Mass at Christ the King Seminary Chapel when, from out of nowhere, a man suddenly approached me and asked "Excuse me, Sir, are you depressed?" I looked at him with a smile and answered: "No."

The man insisted, "But you look depressed."

"Well," I said, "I may have my share of problems but I am certainly not depressed!"

Then, I finally got it! The man was the driver sent by the Sisters to fetch the priest who would say Mass in their convent. And what he was asking all along was, "Are you the priest?"

A MOMENT WITH THE LORD

Lord, help me not to be depressed but to see Your smile in every face, in every situation and in everything I encounter. Amen.

A MOMENT WITH THE WORD

"A joyful heart is the health of the body, but a depressed spirit dries up the bones."

Proverbs 17:22

Balete Drive moment

I was rushing to my noontime radio program at Radio Veritas, when I saw a shaggy- looking man writhing in pain at the sidewalk of Balete Drive. He was holding on to his stomach. I had second thoughts about stopping for him because I would surely be late for my radio program.

"What the heck," I said to myself. I turned around and gave the man some money. However, he said he needed some medicines immediately to relieve the pain. I ended up going back to the seminary to get the medicines he needed.

I did not make it on time for my radio program, but the story of the Good Samaritan became so real for me that day at Balete Drive.

A MOMENT WITH THE LORD

Lord, help me to concretize in my life that every person is worth stopping for. Amen.

A MOMENT WITH THE WORD

"I assure you, as often as you did it for my least brothers, you did it for me."

Matthew 25:40

Can priests marry?

There was this priest who was very advanced in his knowledge of Theology. He was, so to speak, "way ahead of his time." One day, he was asked the question: "Can priests marry?" to which he answered, "Well, if they love each other, why not?"

A MOMENT WITH THE LORD

Lord, let not life's twists and turns catch me off-guard. Like a child, let me always be open to the many surprises of life. Amen.

A MOMENT WITH THE WORD

"Set your hearts on the things that are in heaven..."
Colossians 3:1-2

Traeh Dercas

C an you figure out the title of this page? No?
Try reading it in reverse. Got it? Sacred Heart!
The reason we often cannot see or recognize the Sacred Heart is because our priorities and values are inverted.

Needless to say, you cannot see what is sacred if your sight is dead set on the worldly and profane. Neither can you see the heart nor appreciate matters of the heart if you operate mostly from the head and from the pocket.

A MOMENT WITH THE LORD

Lord, teach me what is really important and what really matters in this life. Amen.

A MOMENT WITH THE WORD

"Set your heart first on the Kingdom and justice of God..."

Matthew 6:33

KISS

As you go through life, don't forget to KISS (Keep It Simple, STUPID!)

Don't complicate your life, your relationships, your lifestyle. Simple is beautiful, right?

Make your life simple and peaceful by keeping these attitudes in mind:

Gratitude for the past. Be grateful for everything and everyone, good or bad, in your past.

Trust in the future. Learn to surrender all your plans and worries to the Father.

Love in the present. Do your best now in expressing your love and you will have no regrets about the past.

A MOMENT WITH THE LORD

Lord, help me to live simply, to love much, and to laugh often. Amen.

A MOMENT WITH THE WORD

"Come, I will lead you into solitude, and there, I will speak tenderly to your heart."

Hosea 2:14

June

Our Lady of Naju

'Gamu-gamo'

L ate one evening, while preparing for our comprehensive examinations in Theology, I saw this *gamu-gamo* (winged ant) crawling at my table. I observed how it crawled.

Whenever it would reach the edge of the table, it would stop, move backwards and go to another direction, until it reached the end of the table again.

The *gamu-gamo* did the same thing twice, thrice. However, on the fourth time, it did something different. It spread its wings and flew away, free.

Finally!

A MOMENT WITH THE LORD

Lord, take away my fears and insecurities. Give me the courage to break loose from my bondages. Help me to conquer sin and pride in my life. Amen.

A MOMENT WITH THE WORD

"I will bear you! It is I who have done this, I who will continue, and I who will carry you to safety."

Isaiah 46:4

I had only one son

How generous are you to God?

A friend of mine thought she was. She goes to Mass everyday, gets involved in parish activities, and even does charitable work, until one day, the Lord asked her for her only son.

"I have only one son, and I do not think I would allow my son to become a priest." These were her thoughts as she went to Tagaytay to attend my ordination. But, as she entered the Chapel, she saw the life-size crucifix and right there and then, she felt the presence of God and a voice that asked her, "How about me? I had only one Son, and I gave Him up for you..."

My friend, realizing the generosity of God, prayed in tears, "Lord, I am sorry for my selfishness. If you want my son, then I am entrusting him to you!"

A MOMENT WITH THE LORD

Lord, all too often I take you for granted in my life. Forgive me for my selfishness and lack of generosity to You and to Your people. Amen.

A MOMENT WITH THE WORD

"For God so loved the world He gave His only Son."

John 3:16

Christs the King

An old woman called me up one morning and said she wanted to visit me at Christ the King Seminary. I gave her instructions on how to find the place. I told her she can not miss it, because Christ the King comes right after St. Luke's Hospital. She did not arrive that morning.

In the afternoon, I received another call from the same woman. She sounded tired and discouraged.

"Father Orbos, where is Christ the King? We already passed by St. Luke's and we saw Burger King, then Tapa King , Goto King and then Chowking. But we couldn't find Christ the King!"

I said, laughing, "Lola, don't be discouraged. Just keep on walking and keep on seeking and soon you will see Christ the King!"

A MOMENT WITH THE LORD

Lord, help me to keep focused on You amidst the many distractions in this world. You are my King. Claim me once more as Your own. Amen.

A MOMENT WITH THE WORD

"Seek first his kingship over you, his way of holiness and all these things will be given to you besides."

Matthew 6:33

I will wait for you

My grandmother, the mother of Mama, was a very prayerful and Marian person. Every time we'd visit her in San Carlos, Pangasinan, she would ask me, "Jerry, how many more years before you become a priest?" I would answer: 15 more years, 12 more years, 5 more years and so on. Every time I'd tell her how many more years before my ordination, she would always say with a smile, "I'll wait for you..." And she did! She literally did! My grandmother died at the age of 96 on October 25, 1980, the very same day I was ordained a priest at the Divine Word Seminary, Tagaytay. I was ordained about 10:00 in the morning, and Bai Tinay, my grandmother, died about 3:00 in the afternoon.

My first Mass was a funeral Mass for a woman who prayed for me, encouraged me, and waited for me to become a priest.

A MOMENT WITH THE LORD

Lord, through the years, You have manifested your concrete signs and wonders in my life. You are a God who is real, and your presence in my life is real. Amen.

A MOMENT WITH THE WORD

"I know that you can do everything, nothing is impossible."

John 42:2

Lessons from the ants

ake some moments and learn from the ants. With their heavy load, they make it a point to stop and greet one another. You know what they tell one another? "Carry on, you are doing well!" They ENCOURAGE one another. They do not put down each other.

There is yet one lesson we can learn from the ants: I have never seen a group of ants sitting around, playing cards, or taking it easy while the others are working. They all work hard, and they work together as a team.

A MOMENT WITH THE LORD

Lord, help me not be stingy with praise and affirmation, and help me to appreciate the value of work and the beauty of teamwork. Amen.

A MOMENT WITH THE WORD

"Help carry one another's burden; in this way you will fulfill the law of Christ.

Galatians 6:2

Let it play

Maybe you have one with you right now. Take a moment to look at a cassette player/recorder and you will see the following buttons: PAUSE, STOP/ EJECT, FORWARD, REWIND, PLAY, RECORD.

The problem with many of us is that we keep on pressing the FORWARD and REWIND buttons in our life, and that is the reason why we do not PLAY wonderful music. Let it play, and let God PLAY in your life! As the Blessed Mother said: "Thy will be done!" LET IT PLAY! And please do not forget the button PAUSE – take time to PRAY.

As for the button STOP/EJECT, that is not for you to touch. That is reserved for God. He holds the RECORD button, too, do not forget that.

A MOMENT WITH THE LORD

Lord, help me not to interfere with Your plans. Let Your plans play... let Your will be done in my life. Amen.

A MOMENT WITH THE WORD

"..I am the servant of the Lord. Let it be done to me as you say..."

Luke 1:38

Mag-beer muna tayo!

Yes, you've read it right. I am highly recommending BEER everyday.

B – Bible

Some people are physically big, but their souls are "malnourished" because they do not feed on the Word of God.

E – Eucharist

Some people do not bother anymore to attend the Mass and visit the Blessed Sacrament. Attending the Mass is a refreshing and invigorating act for the soul.

E – Expressions of Love

Never let a day pass by without expressing your love to the Creator and to the people around you.

R – Rosary

Through the rosary, consecrate everything to the Blessed Mother and be assured of her motherly care and protection.

A MOMENT WITH THE LORD

Lord, teach me to live and to love one day at a time. Help me not to deprive myself of the spiritual nourishment I need everyday. Amen.

A MOMENT WITH THE WORD

"Stop drinking water only. Take a little wine for the good of your stomach, and because of your frequent illnesses."

I Timothy 5:23

Useless?

I heard the story that a group of women recently held a meeting to help the tsunami victims. Aside from raising funds, they also decided to bring to their next meeting, whatever useless things they had around in their houses.

Guess what?

In the next meeting they all turned up with their husbands.

A MOMENT WITH THE LORD

Lord, remind me that no one is useless in your sight. Amen.

A MOMENT WITH THE WORD

"...because you are precious to me and because I love you and give you honor."

Isaiah 43:4

The five P's

Someone once told me, that when Peter started to sink while walking on the water, Jesus was supposed to have said "Oh, you man of little feet!"

Levity aside, there are 5 P's that make us heavy and make us sink in this life:

PERA - If we put money above God and people, we may end up heavy with sin, guilt, selfishness and vanity.

POWER – Those who need to throw their weight around are never at ease or at peace.

PRIDE – The proud carry their heavy hearts of stone that have no room for humility and warmth.

PLEASURE – Those who wallow in the lures and pleasures of this world do not want to get going anywhere, not even to heaven, because their only destination is self-destruction.

PROBLEM – Those who are so focused on their own personal burdens and miseries instead of being focused on Jesus will sink, like Peter.

A MOMENT WITH THE LORD

Lord, keep me focused on You so as not to sink. Amen.

A MOMENT WITH THE WORD

"Everything is lawful for me – but that does not mean that everything is good for me..."

1 Corinthians 6:12

Successful

Are you a successful person? Congratulations! But, are you a significant person?

A successful person is one who earns and accumulates wealth or honors for himself. On the other hand, a significant person is one who, with or without wealth or honors, affects positively the people around him/her.

Indeed, a person is worth not for what he/she has, not even for who he/she is, but, for what others have become because of him/her.

A MOMENT WITH THE LORD

Lord, help me to live a significant life. Amen.

A MOMENT WITH THE WORD

"Be an example for the believers in your speech, your conduct, your love, faith and purity."

I Timothy 4:12

The handkerchief and the necktie

Take a moment to look at the lowly handkerchief... a very small thing, hidden in the pocket most of the time, but very useful and very handy for wiping away tears and perspiration.

What about the necktie? The necktie is very visible, very prominent. But what is the necktie for? Not much really. Just for decoration, for display. Nothing more. Quite opposite of the lowly handkerchief.

So what would you rather be: a handkerchief or a necktie?

A MOMENT WITH THE LORD

Lord, help me to be like the Blessed Mother – humble, hidden, but doing everything with much love. May I be a "handkerchief" to others. Amen.

A MOMENT WITH THE WORD

"Be on guard against performing religious acts for people to see. Otherwise, expect no recompense from your heavenly Father."

Matthew 6:1

Believe like a child

What does a child believe in? I would like to share with you a song I made for Fatima Soriano, a 14-year-old blind girl and a kidney transplantee, who is an inspiration because of her simple faith, joy and trust. It's title is "Believe, Like A Child":

I believe in miracles; I believe in "impossibles"; I believe in love and blessings from above; I believe in God; I believe God will provide; I believe He's at my side; I believe He knows my wishes and desires; yes I believe in God; I believe in letting go, and letting God; I believe in letting be and letting God be God; Yes I believe, I believe in God. I believe He has a plan. I believe His hidden hand. I believe He's doing everything He can, and I believe He can; I believe things will be fine; I believe all in His time; I believe and trust He has a big surprise, yes I believe I am His child.

A MOMENT WITH THE LORD

Lord, help me to believe and keep on believing like a child. Amen.

A MOMENT WITH THE WORD

"Let the children come to me and do not hinder them. It is to the just such as these that the kingdom of God belongs."

Mark 10:14

The missed train

There is a story about three men who were drunk. They were out to catch the last train which was already pulling out of the station. The three tried to run and catch up with the train. The train conductor pulled in the first, and then the second. But he failed when he tried to pull in the third. So the third man was left behind.

The station master commiserates with the man who was left behind. But the man said, "Well, I am sorry for those guys. You see, they were here just to see me off!"

A MOMENT WITH THE LORD

Lord, help me not to miss the most important person in my life...You, and the most important thing in my life... love! Amen.

A MOMENT WITH THE WORD

"What profit does a man show who gains the whole world and destroys himself in the process?"

Mark 8:36

The monkey and the coconut

Here is a story I heard about how people trap monkeys.

Food is placed inside an empty coconut shell. The monkey would put its hand into the shell through a little hole and would grab the food. But when it would pull out its hand, it would not fit through the hole anymore because of its closed fist holding the food.

If only it would let go of the food, the monkey could go away freely. But the monkey would not let go, and so it was easily trapped.

What are those things you cannot let go? Is it your pride, your sins, your vices, your riches? These are the things that "trap you."

A MOMENT WITH THE LORD

Lord, as I go in life, may my hands be more open in giving and in sharing. Let me give, Lord, while I live. Amen.

A MOMENT WITH THE WORD

"The needy will never be lacking in the land; that is why I command you to open your hand to your poor and needy kinsman in your country."

Deuteronomy 15:11

The shattered crucifix

Have you ever tried to take a closer look at the crucifix?

There was once an old man who was dying. He called his three sons and divided his properties. To the eldest son, he gave the house. To the second son, he gave the farm. To the youngest son, he said: "You are most precious to me, my son. To you I give this crucifix..." The man breathed his last, leaving the youngest son with so much anger, resentment and envy.

One night, in a fit of anger, he grabbed the crucifix and threw it to the floor. The crucifix was shattered and broken into tiny, shining pieces. Lo and behold, inside the crucifix were many precious jewels and stones hidden by the father: "You are most precious to me, my son. To you I give this crucifix..."

A MOMENT WITH THE LORD

Lord, the crosses that You send my way are my jewels in this life and in the life to come. Help me, Lord, to embrace the cross. Help me, Lord, to embrace You. Amen.

A MOMENT WITH THE WORD

"Whoever wishes to be my follower must deny his very self, take up his cross each day, and follow my steps."

Luke 9:23

The smell of roses

After the consecration at Mass with about twenty ex-seminarians (XVDs) present, I smelled the fragrance of roses, which, as you know, is a manifestation of the Blessed Mother's presence. We were on an island when it happened. There were no roses around. There was no wind at all.

After some moments of silence, I asked the group if they smelled the fragrance of roses, and almost everyone said they did. Then, in tears, I told the group what the scent of rose meant.

That moment, I knew the Blessed Mother was around. She was telling us that God was embracing each one of us. Mama Mary, in a single moment, manifested God's unconditional love. That night, I witnessed big men shed tears of repentance and gratitude in a candle-lit chapel in an island somewhere in Pangasinan.

A MOMENT WITH THE LORD

Lord, You use all means to reach out to me. Thank you for not giving up on me. Thank you for Your mother who always brings us closer to You. Amen.

A MOMENT WITH THE WORD

"Thanks be to God for His indescribable gift!"
2 Corinthians 9:15

Learning a new language

Learning the Korean language can be an unforgettable experience.

There was this missionary who was giving advice to a penitent, and when he came to the penance, he wanted to say *"Pajim opshi, mokju se pon haseyo"* (which meant, without fail, say the rosary three times), but instead, he said *"Paji opshi, mekju se pon haseyo"* (which meant, without pants, drink beer three times!)

It is not easy to be a missionary. It is a big sacrifice to leave one's country and to learn a new language and live in a new culture.

But then, nothing is heavy if the heart is light.

Nothing is cold, if the heart is warm.

Indeed we can do anything, and we will do everything for Christ!

A MOMENT WITH THE LORD

Lord, it is only You who knows the things I do and what I go through for love of You. Amen.

A MOMENT WITH THE WORD

"In him who is the source of my strength I have strength for everything."

Philippians 4:13

Worms

A visionary once vividly described how big and live worms come out from the mouth of a person who is used to lying, cursing, gossiping or maligning others.

The worms according to the visionary, are strong. They spread fast. The only way to stop them is when an apology is made or a lie is corrected.

So, next time you are tempted to lie, curse, gossip or malign others, think about it again. And when you have offended others through your mouth's carelessness, never give a second thought about asking for an apology or correcting a lie. Always remember the worms.

A MOMENT WITH THE LORD

Lord, let my mouth be a source of fragrant thanksgiving praise to You, and a source of love and truth for others. Amen.

A MOMENT WITH THE WORD

"A guard on the mouth makes life secure..."

Proverbs 13:3

'Medugorean'

Question: What do you call a person who has been to Medugorje?

Answer: Medugorean.

Question: What do you call an old person who has been to Medugorje?

Answer: *Medyo gorang!*

A MOMENT WITH THE LORD

Lord, when people call me this and that, remind me that what matters most is what you call me and who I am to your heart. Amen.

A MOMENT WITH THE WORD

"I shall not call you servant anymore... instead I have called you friends..."

John 15:15

A bloated moment

In one party I attended, I met this guy who was highly opinionated and who had such a big ego. He kept talking about himself, his achievements and what people say about him. I just kept quiet, listening to his monologue. After some moments, he sort of noticed that he was monopolizing the conversation, and so he tells me, "Oh, how about you Father Orbos... what can you say, about me?!" Wow! For some people it's just really I, me, and myself all the way!

A MOMENT WITH THE LORD

Lord, help me to realize that there's more to this world than I, me, and myself. Amen.

A MOMENT WITH THE WORD

"And they are greedy as dogs, never satisfied...all of them intent on personal gain."

Isaiah 56:11

The poor rich man

Remember the story of a poor and a rich man who were shipwrecked together? Who do you think survived? The poor man survived because his hands were free, while the rich man drowned because he held on and would not let go of his two bags so full of money and pieces of jewelry.

If only he gave one of his bags to the poor man...but no, selfish as he was, he held on to his riches and wealth down to his watery grave.

If only he gave one of his bags... he could have helped a poor man, and he could have saved his life, he could have even saved his soul...

A MOMENT WITH THE LORD

Lord, are my hands so full that I can no longer hold on to you? Open my heart. Amen.

A MOMENT WITH THE WORD

"...those who are stingy will lose everything."

Proverbs 11:24

A humbling moment

Sometime in the early 80s, I was at a small bus stop waiting for a ride going to Abra. I was drinking my early morning coffee in a quiet corner when a jeepload of soldiers arrived. One of them who was drunk approached me. When he found out that I was a priest, he started letting out his grievances against the church and priests, at times pointing his armalite rifle at me. Those were tense and scary moments. Through it all, I swallowed my pride and kept my cool. (Wasn't persecution and even martyrdom a part of a priest's life after all?) I was shaking, not so much because of fear, but because of anger. How many small and helpless people are persecuted and humiliated by government people who are drunk and loaded with power?

Somehow, I still managed to say "God bless you" as he was brought away.

A MOMENT WITH THE LORD

Lord, how many times must I forgive my brother who sins against me? At times it is not easy Lord. Amen.

A MOMENT WITH THE WORD

"Love your enemies. Pray for those who persecute you."
Matthew 5:44

No regrets

June 23, 1987 was a very sad day in my life.

It was the day when my father died. I miss my father. In fact, the pain is never really gone. I look forward to seeing him and embracing him again in heaven. While there is pain, I have no regrets whenever I think of my late father.

Why? Because I really loved him as much as I could while he was still alive. I really did my best for him.

I knew that. And he knew that, too.

A MOMENT WITH THE LORD

Lord, help me to live with much love so that I won't have much regrets in life. Amen.

A MOMENT WITH THE WORD

"Teach us how short life is, so that we may become wise."

Psalm 90:12

A whole lifetime

The only brother of my paternal grandmother boarded a boat for America when he was only a teenager, and promised never to come back. He was hurt and resentful because his parents would not let him study. For years nothing was heard from him except occasional letters to my father with some dollars to help him finish law school.

In 1978, my father made his first trip to America in search for his lost uncle. He searched everywhere until finally he found him in some grape plantation somewhere in California. Uncle and nephew embraced and cried unashamedly. Finally he was convinced to come home. A Christmas reunion was set in the Philippines... but he died a few months before that.

So sad... a whole lifetime in pain and hurting. All because of a resentful and an unforgiving heart.

A MOMENT WITH THE LORD

Lord, remove all my pains, hurts, and "tampo" in my heart. Amen.

A MOMENT WITH THE WORD

"Do not nurse hatred in your heart for any of your relatives...do not seek revenge or nurture a grudge against one of your people..."

Leviticus 19:17-18

Abortion

At a Mass in Lourdes with Filipino pilgrims, Julia, the visionary from Korea felt stomach pains, sweating like a woman in labor. Before our very eyes, the stomach of Julia became enlarged. I asked her what was happening. (Julia, as you know, is a victim-soul who suffers for other people and who gives the Blessed Mother's messages). She told me (I speak Korean) that there was somebody in the church who just had an abortion, and she was experiencing the pains of a fetus being aborted. The Blessed Mother was using her body to express her message of true repentance and true penance for the sin of abortion. I prayed over her, and before our very eyes her stomach became smaller and smaller.

After the Mass, I saw a woman embracing Julia, crying like a child in the arms of her mother.

A MOMENT WITH THE LORD

Lord, remind me that every child is precious, every life has a purpose. Amen.

A MOMENT WITH THE WORD

"Even before I formed you in the womb, I knew you... and consecrated you..."

Jeremiah 1:15

'Allah!'

How strong is your faith in Christ?

The story is told of a Buddhist, a Muslim, and a Christian who were debating whose God is the greatest. To settle the issue once and for all, they decided to jump from a 20-storey building and find out whose God will save them. First, the Buddhist shouts "Buddha!", jumps, and lands on the ground dead in a few seconds. The Muslim shouts "Allah!", jumps, and wonder of wonders, is carried by a wind and landed safely.

It was the Christian's turn. With all trust he shouts "Jesus Christ, in you I entrust my life!" and jumps. As he was falling past the 6th, 5th, and 4th floors, and nothing was happening, he was last heard shouting "Allah! Allah! Allah *eh!* Allah *na!*"

A MOMENT WITH THE LORD

Lord, give me a strong faith and help me to really entrust my whole life unto you. Amen.

A MOMENT WITH THE WORD

"If we endure, we shall also reign with Him. If we deny Him, He also will deny us."

2 Timothy 2:10

From sacristan to bishop

Fr. Leopoldo Jaucian, SVD, was ordained bishop at Christ the King Seminary, in the very church where he served as a lowly, diligent sacristan before he entered the seminary. It is his humility that has endeared him to so many people. Even as our provincial superior, he was very understanding and welcomed confreres with open arms. These are the very same traits that make him effective and efficacious in the Diocese of Abra. *"Manete in me"* (Remain in me) is his motto. Bishop Pol is Bishop Pol because he has truly, humbly and conscientiously remained in God.

A MOMENT WITH THE LORD

Lord, amidst trials and challenges, help me to remain in You. Amen.

A MOMENT WITH THE WORD

"Remain in me as I in you...I am the vine, you are the branches."

John 15:4-5

An elevator moment

Roby Montellano, a member of the XVD (an association of SVD ex- seminarians) related to me his unforgettable experience of being trapped with 6 people in an elevator for some 45 minutes, which he said seemed like eternity. At first he thought it would just be a matter of minutes before the power would be restored, but it dragged on. It was dark. Only the glow from their cellphones provided some light. And it was hot. Soon two of his companions passed out. Through it all, he kept giving hope to the others, and kept praying to the Blessed Mother.

Take it from Roby.

There's really nothing one can do at such moments except to pray, hope and hold on.

A MOMENT WITH THE LORD

Lord, in life there is only You, and in the end, there's only You. Amen.

A MOMENT WITH THE WORD

"Cast your burdens on the Lord, and He shall sustain you."

Psalm 55:22

Backhoe moment

E verytime I see it, I shake my head in disbelief and feel sorry for the owner of a backhoe half submerged in a beach somewhere in Pangasinan. From what I heard, the owner of this expensive machine ventured to do some dredging during the low tide. Then it developed engine trouble. They tried, but they could not fix it on time. The tide set in, and it was submerged in sea water. It still sits there, this million peso machine, useless and rusty overtaken by the tide, overtaken by events.

A MOMENT WITH THE LORD

Lord, help me to be vigilant and wise so that I will not be overtaken by the circumstances, and by the tides of life. Amen.

A MOMENT WITH THE WORD

"My son, hold on to sound judgement and discretion and do not let them out of your sight."

Proverbs 3:21

Be good to yourself

Angry? Hurt? Cannot forgive?

Perhaps we can borrow the wisdom of the late Senator and poet, Francisco "Soc" Rodrigo who said: *"Nandoon ako, galit na galit, nagngingitngit, nang nalaman ko na lang na ang kaaway ko, tulog na tulog at naghihilik!"* Translated loosely, it means, "There I was so full of anger and hate, only to find out that my enemy was sleeping soundly, snoring even in his sleep!"

Anger and hate will do you no good.

Be good to yourself. Forgive.

A MOMENT WITH THE LORD

Lord, help me to forgive, so that my joy will be complete. Amen.

A MOMENT WITH THE WORD

"When you follow the desires of your sinful nature, your lives will produce these evil results..."

Galatians 5:19

July

Our Lady of Mount Carmel

Bottomline

What is the bottom line?

The bottom line is when you are there lying in the coffin and people will come to see you for the last time. What will people remember about you...? What will your family and loved ones feel and remember about you...? Finally, what will your God and Creator say to you when you come face to face with Him? That is the bottom line. Nothing else follows.

A MOMENT WITH THE LORD

Lord, help me to live a life that is full, beautiful, meaningful, love-full and God-full. Amen.

A MOMENT WITH THE WORD

"Teach us to number our days, that we may gain a heart of wisdom..."

Psalm 90:12

Bro. Daniel

Bro. Daniel, an SVD missionary from Germany never said much, never gave conferences nor taught in classes, but, to this very day, whenever I remember my seminary days, I still carry in my heart his message of simplicity, humility, hard work, and deep religious commitment by his life example. He did the dirtiest and the most humbling work – that of taking care of our pigs. After our meals, he would collect with his hands the leftover food, and he did it all with so much joy and humility.

On his 50th anniversary, we called him up the stage to say something. For a while, he stood there, not quite knowing what to do. We realized all the more, his hiddenness and simplicity when he said, "Please excuse me. It's my first time to speak before a crowd and my first time to use a microphone."

A MOMENT WITH THE LORD

Lord, indeed they say little who love much. Help me to talk less, and love more. Amen.

A MOMENT WITH THE WORD

"If anyone desires to be first, he shall be the last of all and servant of all."

Mark 9:35

Carry no trash

Where in the world would you see passenger trains carrying trash and garbage as well? Only in the Philippines! By the time a PNR train reaches its main terminal in Tutuban, its roof would be full of plastic bags of garbage and trash thrown from homes along the "riles" (railroad tracks). But that was before. Now, our PNR trains have been remodeled with triangular roofs so that any trash or garbage thrown into it would not stay. Yes our trains carry no trash no more!

Galing ng Pinoy, ano?

Sana, ikaw rin. Carry no trash.

A MOMENT WITH THE LORD

Lord, remove all the trash and garbage in my heart and in my life. Amen.

A MOMENT WITH THE WORD

"When you pass through deep waters I will be with you... Your trouble will not overwhelm you."

Isaiah 43:2

Crisis management

Did you hear about this guy who was good in giving instant remedies and palliatives in solving problems?

His cows would not eat the brown grass because of the drought. What did he do? He put green sunglasses on the cows. Problem solved!

He always forgets his driving eyeglasses, so what did he do? He had the whole windshield graded. Problem solved! But sorry for those who ride, and feel dizzy in his car.

A MOMENT WITH THE LORD

Lord, when my soul is sick, let me seek you and not the shallow solutions and palliatives of this world. Amen.

A MOMENT WITH THE WORD

"...Set your heart on seeking God."

2 Chronicles 19:3

Funny

The e-mail message says "FUNNY... how P1,000 look so big in church, but how small in the mall... how long a couple of hours is in the church but how short when watching a movie... how we get thrilled at overtime or extra innings, but we complain when a sermon is extended... how hard it is to read the Bible but how easy it is to read a novel... how people scramble for front seats in a game but stay at the back of the church... how hard to put a church event in our schedule, but how easy to adjust for other events..."

We can add more "funny" lines, but, the message is clear. We tend to take the Lord and our spiritual life for granted because we have more "important matters" to attend to. Actually, there's nothing "funny" about that.

A MOMENT WITH THE LORD

Lord, help me not to belittle those that are really important in life. Amen.

A MOMENT WITH THE WORD

"Do not be like the horse or like the mule, which have no understanding."

Psalm 32:9

Giver or taker?

Take a moment to look at your hands. Are you a giver or a taker?

As you go through life, are your hands open or are they closed? Ever wonder why you don't seem to receive blessings from God? Maybe it is because your hands are closed. Remember that you can receive only if your hands are open.

Congratulations to all of you givers out there. As someone put it, givers have open hands and open hearts. There may be times when their hands are empty, but their hearts will always be full!

A MOMENT WITH THE LORD

Lord, while I live, let me give and give, and give. Amen.

A MOMENT WITH THE WORD

"God has given gifts to each one of you... manage them well so that God's generosity can flow through you."

I Peter 4:10

Go back

How deep is your love, your commitment? Here are two text messages which I would like to share to husbands and wives out there.

Text 1:

Husband is asked what his gift is to his wife on their 25th wedding anniversary. "I will take her for a trip to Africa." And on their 50th wedding anniversary? "I will fetch her from Africa!"

Text 2:

Husband is teary eyed and wife asks him what's wrong? Husband says, "Remember 22 years ago, I got you pregnant and your Dad said either I marry you or go to jail? Well, I was just computing... I would have been released today!"

Go back, keep going back to your original love and commitment. Hold on, persevere through it all till you come before your Creator and can say, "Mission accomplished!"

A MOMENT WITH THE LORD

Lord, keep the flame of love alive in my heart. Amen.

A MOMENT WITH THE WORD

"God blesses the people who patiently endure testing. Afterwards they will receive the crown of life that God has promised to those who love Him."

James 1:12

Goldfish and spiders

I remember two moments of childhood greed and selfishness.

The first one was when somebody gave me a dozen fighting spiders from the barrio one afternoon. Oh how my friends wooed me to give some to them, but no, I kept them all in matchboxes in a secret place which I thought no one else could find out... except for the ants who feasted on them that night...

The other moment was when a friend of Papa gave me a dozen goldfish which I put in a little aquarium. I remember how my cousin was asking me to give him even only one for his aquarium, but I refused. All of them were mine! And all of them were still mine the next morning, all twelve of them, floating dead.

A MOMENT WITH THE LORD

Lord, help me to be generous. Remove greed from my heart. Amen.

A MOMENT WITH THE WORD

"And they are greedy as dogs, never satisfied... all of them intent on personal gain."

Isaiah 56:11

Haircut

Having a haircut always gives me a nice feeling. It is one of those times when I who minister a lot, feel and allow myself to be ministered to by others. It is an acceptance and expression of my need for others, my littleness, and dependence.

It is also like going to God and saying "Okay Lord, here I am. Take over, cut away all those unruly and unyielding bad habits!" And when I get that parting massage on my neck and shoulders, it is like being affirmed by God who is saying "You're ok. You're all right. Get going. I am with you!"

A MOMENT WITH THE LORD

Lord, continue to cut and trim me, and my wild and unruly ways. Amen.

A MOMENT WITH THE WORD

"As clay in the potter's hands so are you in my hands."
Jeremiah 18:6

Humble and humbling

"How are you, *Manong!*" I called out to Fr. Artemio Rillera, as I arrived at the Mission House in Bangued, Abra. He was sweeping the floor in his white T-shirt, humble and unassuming and, as always, welcoming.

After our greetings, I told my driver to bring my bags to the second floor. After I left, my driver called Fr. Rillera to help him bring up my bags, thinking that he was the gardener or the janitor of the place. *Manong* humbly and dutifully obliged. Imagine the embarrassment of my driver when he found out later that "Fr. *Manong* Rillera" was the Provincial Superior of the SVD Northern Province!

By the way, he is not the provincial anymore. He is now bishop of La Union.

A MOMENT WITH THE LORD

Lord, help me never to judge or underestimate people just by their external appearances and situations. Amen.

A MOMENT WITH THE WORD

"Whoever humbles himself as this little child is the greatest in the Kingdom of Heaven."

Matthew 18:4

Live tourists

While driving to Pangasinan with my little nephews and nieces, it so happened that we were following a tricycle with two pigs in it. I did not give it much thought till one of my nieces said: "Look how good the owner is to be bringing around his pigs for a ride and for sight seeing!"

I saw the pigs, and saw nothing but dead meat for the market, while my niece saw live tourists!

A MOMENT WITH THE LORD

Lord, open my heart and my eyes to keep seeing your goodness, beauty and love. Amen.

A MOMENT WITH THE WORD

"A good person produces good words from a good heart, and an evil person produces evil words from an evil heart."
Matthew 12:35

Shake it off

Here is a parable I heard, about an old mule that fell on a deep, dry well. As it was impossible to lift it up, the farmer decided to bury it right there and then. Together with his neighbors, they started filling up the well with soil and dirt. At first, the mule panicked that he was going to be buried alive. But soon he discovered that every time soil and dirt would fall on its back, he could shake it off, and step up. He continued to just shake it off and step up, until the well was full. Exhausted but happy, the mule finally stepped over the well and walked away free amidst the cheering crowd, because it knew how to shake it off, rise up, and get going.

A MOMENT WITH THE LORD

Lord, I don't have to carry my burdens because I can always cast them upon you! Amen.

A MOMENT WITH THE WORD

"Come to me all of you...who carry heavy burdens and I will refresh you."

Matthew 11:28

Simple colds

Now I know why we call it simple colds...

It was a long, full Monday ending with my 11:00 pm radio program at Radio Veritas. Aside from that, I had fever and colds, and all I wanted to do was to go home, and sleep.

But guess what? A woman wanted to talk to me. At 11:30 pm? At first, I could not hide my irritation and hesitance, but still managed to say yes with a faint smile. Soon all my fatigue and pains vanished as I listened with compassion to this woman who just lost her 11-year-old son in a freak accident.

I was feeling miserable with my simple colds, and here she was, grieving for an only son...

How simple indeed are our troubles compared to those of others.

A MOMENT WITH THE LORD

Lord, help me not to forget that there are people who have bigger problems and burdens than me. Amen.

A MOMENT WITH THE WORD

"You must be compassionate, just as your Father is compassionate."

Luke 6:36

The bangar tree

When we were children, there was a bangar tree at the back of our school. Most of the time, it was just there unnoticed. But, in the summer it makes its presence felt because of its beautiful red orange flowers in full bloom. What a sight! But, it also makes its presence felt because of its foul odor. What a smell!

Mama and Papa would often take the occasion to remind us that there is more to life than external beauty; What is more important in life is the sweet fragrance of character.

A MOMENT WITH THE LORD

Lord, give me a beautiful heart that is pleasing to you. Amen.

A MOMENT WITH THE WORD

"Charm is deceptive, and beauty does not last; but a woman who fears the Lord will be greatly praised."

Proverbs 31:30

Unmasked

There is a story about a jobless man who finally got a job in a circus, playing the part of a gorilla. Every day he delighted the crowd with his twisting and turning.

One day, he slipped and fell into the lion's cage and he began to scream, "Help! Get me out of here!"

The lion came up to him and said: "Be quiet, you fool, or we'll both lose our jobs."

A MOMENT WITH THE LORD

Lord, help me to remove all the masks I put on in this life just to survive. Amen.

A MOMENT WITH THE WORD

"Your hands have made me and fashioned me; give me discernment that I may learn your commands."

Psalm 119:73

Widow's mite

A woman walked into my office one day. She said she heard me over the radio appealing for prayers and financial help for our Filipino missionaries abroad, and here she was to make a little donation. From her bag she took a little brown paper bag full of coins. It was, she said, the collection *(abuloy)* from her late husband's wake, and she was giving it all...

In shame, and almost in tears, I accepted the money, truly and literally, a widow's mite.

A MOMENT WITH THE LORD

Lord, remind me that you appreciate every and any little thing I do. Amen.

A MOMENT WITH THE WORD

"The poor widow came along and dropped in two little copper coins...poor as she is... she gave all she had to live on."

Mark 12:42-44

Word alive

The story is told about a father who brought his son to church to attend Mass. The little boy had many questions about the rituals and the movements of the priest, and the father patiently explained everything to him. During the homily which went on and on, the little boy saw the priest look at his watch and asked his father what that meant. His exasperated reply was, "It means nothing at all, son, nothing at all."

A MOMENT WITH THE LORD

Lord, make your word alive in me, and use me to bring your living words to others. Amen.

A MOMENT WITH THE WORD

"Then the Lord reached out, touched my lips, and said to me, ...listen, I am giving you the words you must speak."
Jeremiah 1:9

A Chinese proverb

hink about it: "He who blames others has a long way to go on his journey. He who blames himself is halfway there. He who blames no one has arrived."

A MOMENT WITH THE LORD

Lord, help me to realize that when I blame, I become lame. Amen.

A MOMENT WITH THE WORD

"Do everything without complaining or arguing."
Philippians 2:14

Carry your cross

Remember the story of a man who went to heaven? St. Peter called him to an anteroom filled with so many crosses of different colors and different shades. St. Peter told him to choose which cross he would like to carry if he were to go back to earth and live again. He took a long time to choose. Finally, he pointed at a cross in one corner. St. Peter asked him, "Is that your final answer? Sure?" When he said yes, St. Peter told him, "My child, don't you know that **that** was the very same cross you were carrying while you were still on earth, and you were always complaining and complaining?"

The lesson of the story is that instead of complaining, you should take up whatever cross you have now and trust in the Lord who has given you that cross. He knows that you can handle it.

A MOMENT WITH THE LORD

Lord, may the cross I carry help me become a better, not a bitter person. Amen.

A MOMENT WITH THE WORD

"Whoever wishes to be my follower must deny his very self, take up his cross each day, and follow my steps."

Luke 9:23

A Calasiao accident

Coming from a basketball game with my brother priests late one evening, I thought I saw a lighted candle along the road. I pulled over, and there on the dark sidewalk lay a lifeless body covered with a white sheet. The body was that of a 19-year-old teenage girl, who was run over by a speeding bus some 30 minutes ago. She was coming home to Calasiao, Pangasinan, to attend the birthday of a friend. It turned out to be her birthday in eternity.

A MOMENT WITH THE LORD

Lord, I do not know the time or the hour. Help me to be prepared to meet You anytime. Amen.

A MOMENT WITH THE WORD

"You do not know when the appointed time will come."
Mark 13:33

A 'foto-me' moment

Once, a classmate in the seminary needed an ID picture fast, so I suggested that he go to one of those "Foto-Me" stands. He came back with a story to tell and a set of amazing pictures of himself – looking up, looking down, and looking to the side – and his stomach. What had happened?

He said he was told to sit down and focus on the box in front of him. There was a flash, and he looked up. Another flash, and he looked down. Still another flash, and he looked to the side. Not knowing what to do next, he stood up, and that's when the fourth flash "exposed" his stomach!

A MOMENT WITH THE LORD

Lord, help me to stay focused on You. Help me to avoid being distracted by the world. Help me to avoid embarrassing and even shameful moments in my life, moments when I focus on myself. Amen.

A MOMENT WITH THE WORD

"The man of intelligence fixes his gaze on wisdom, but the eyes of a fool are on the ends of the earth."

Proverbs 17:24

A jellyfish moment

A five-year-old boy, seeing a jellyfish for the first time, was so fascinated by it. Then after observing the jellyfish for some time he exclaimed that it had no face! Why was this so, he asked. Neither his father nor his mother could give an answer.

"Ah," the boy finally said, "maybe God got tired so He did not finish the face. Maybe later on He will."

A MOMENT WITH THE LORD

Lord, help me never to forget the sense of wonder of a child, and help me not to lose the sensitivity and sense of optimism of a child. Amen.

A MOMENT WITH THE WORD

"I assure you that unless you change and become like children, you will never enter the Kingdom of Heaven."
Matthew 18:3

A priestly blessing

I heard this story about a deranged man who climbed a tree, and no one – not the police, the fire department, the mayor, or even his relatives - could make him come down. Finally, the parish priest was called in. He took a long look at the man up in the tree and gave his blessing. To the amazement of many, the man hurriedly came down. Everyone marveled at the power of the priest's blessing.

When asked later why he came down, the deranged man said. "Well, I saw this man in a white robe, who raised his hand. With the vertical and horizontal movement with his hand, he meant to tell me: "You better come down, I'm cutting the tree!"

A MOMENT WITH THE LORD

Lord, may I never underestimate the value and power of every blessing. Amen.

A MOMENT WITH THE WORD

"In the name of the Father, and of the Son, and of the Holy Spirit."

Matthew 28:19

A sweepstakes moment

I remember the stories of Papa about his financial hardships as a law student at U.P. One day, a rich classmate invited him for merienda. As they were eating, a little boy in tattered clothes kept begging him to buy sweepstakes tickets. Taking pity on the boy he bought two sweepstakes tickets with his last money, one for him and one for his friend. At least, he thought, he was somehow repaying his friend's goodness and generosity.

Well, Papa won third prize in the sweepstakes draw, enough to finance his bar review classes! He always told us he was convinced that it was the baby Jesus who had sold him the sweepstakes ticket.

A MOMENT WITH THE LORD

Lord, You always provide. Help me always to abide. Amen.

A MOMENT WITH THE WORD

"Cast all your cares to the Lord for He cares for you."
I Peter 5:7

'... And also with you'

Do you remember the story of the priest who began saying Mass with such solemnity but soon found out that his microphone was not working? He tapped the microphone, and with a loud voice spread his hands and said, "Ah, something's wrong with the mike!" And the whole congregation automatically responded. "And also with you!"

A MOMENT WITH THE LORD

Lord, help me to pray with my heart at every Mass. Amen.

A MOMENT WITH THE WORD

"When you pray, do not be like hypocrites who love to stand and pray in the synagogues and on street corners so that others may see them."

Matthew 6:5

Frozen delights

In Alaska, I had the awesome experience of seeing glaciers. What a sight! A real delight to the eyes. But, glaciers are cold and frozen, yes, "frozen delights" —like some of us, beautiful on the outside but cold and empty, lifeless, loveless, bitter and angry deep inside.

A MOMENT WITH THE LORD

Lord, warm my heart and melt the glaciers in my life so that I do not become a "frozen delight." Amen.

A MOMENT WITH THE WORD

"I will remove the stony heart from their bodies, and replace it with a natural heart."

Ezekiel 11:19

Held by Jesus

The story is told about an atheist couple who had a son. Both parents never told their child anything about God or about Jesus. One night, the couple had a fight where the father shot the mother and then shot himself. It all happened in front of the child. The child was sent to a foster home.

One day, in Sunday school, the teacher held up a picture of Jesus and asked if anyone knew who it was. The child in the story raised his hands and said: "That's the man who was holding me the night my parents died."

A MOMENT WITH THE LORD

Lord, thank you for being with me when I have no one. Amen.

A MOMENT WITH THE WORD

"Even if I go through the deepest darkness, I will not be afraid, Lord, for you are with me."

Psalm 23:4

Prayer works!

I was driving an old jeep on my way to an evening Mass in a remote barrio, with about six children as my "bodyguards." Suddenly the engine stopped. It was an isolated place, and I could not restart the vehicle. Believing and relying only on the power of prayer, I told the children to pray aloud with me for the Lord to help us. But deep in my half-believing heart, I was almost threatening the Lord, saying, "You better fix this, Lord; otherwise, the people will not have Mass tonight." After our short prayer, I switched on the ignition, and the engine restarted!

When we reached the barrio, I did not have to preach. The children themselves told everyone how we had prayed, and how the Lord had answered our prayers!

A MOMENT WITH THE LORD

Lord, help me to be simple and trusting like a child. Amen.

A MOMENT WITH THE WORD

"Unless you become like children, you cannot enter the kingdom of heaven."

Matthew 18:3

Telephones in heaven

Here's an angel story I heard. One day while strolling in heaven, St. Peter passed an angel who was answering calls nonstop on his many telephones. Then, as St. Peter walked on, he passed another angel who also had many telephones but rarely had a phone call.

According to the story, the angel with many telephones and a lot of phone calls is the angel who receives prayer requests and complaints, while the angel with many telephones and few phone calls is the angel who receives thanksgiving prayers from earth.

Which angel do you call often?

A MOMENT WITH THE LORD

Lord, teach me to be grateful and never cease offering prayers of praise and gratitude, no matter what. Amen.

A MOMENT WITH THE WORD

"Rejoice always, never cease praying, render constant thanks: such is God's will for you in Christ Jesus."
                                        Thessalonians 5:16-18

Tenacity

Here's a story I heard about a man driving up to Baguio for the first time. It was dark and foggy. Fortunately there was another car ahead of him. So he decided to follow the car and, in fact, tailgated it through the thick fog.

He was elated with his strategy. Then in the thick fog the car ahead stopped, and when it did not move for some time, he blew his horn. The other driver alighted from his car and asked him what was wrong.

"*Abante na,*" he said. "Let's keep going."

The other driver retorted: "What do you mean, keep going. I'm already in my garage!"

A MOMENT WITH THE LORD

Lord, help me to follow you through thick and thin till I reach heaven. Amen.

A MOMENT WITH THE WORD

"I have given you a model to follow, so that as I have done for you, you should also do."

John 13:15

The 4-H for peace

For a peaceful life, don't forget these four H's:

- **Honesty**. Yes, honesty is still the best policy. An honest person is a person at peace.
- **Humility**. A person finds peace and contentment when he has no airs about himself, when he knows and accepts himself and does not pretend to be something or someone else.
- **Hard Work**. There is no substitute for hard work. You know how empty it feels to be all form and no substance. Are you hard working or hardly working?
- **Holiness**. Follow God's ways and you will have peace. Turn away from God and you will never find peace.
- And one more H – **Humor**! Don't take yourself too seriously. Smile, laugh, and, with childlike confidence trust in our loving Father, who has a terrific sense of humor.

A MOMENT WITH THE LORD

Lord, remind me always to go back to the heart, and there find You. Amen.

A MOMENT WITH THE WORD

"Clothe yourselves with humility in your dealings with one another."

1 Peter 5:5

August

**The Assumption
of the Blessed Virgin Mary**

A brave heart

He was only 21 years old, full of life and love. He was a very good son to a very loving mother. He was contemplating to join the Society of the Divine Word (SVD) in Techny , Illinois to follow God's call.

But tragedy struck when Ryan, my nephew, drowned on August 11, 2002 during a family outing in Vancouver, Canada.

Why him?

Why now?

How come?

It was his mother, my cousin, Linda who answered these questions for me when I talked with her over the phone.

She expressed, "God's will be done. The Lord has called Ryan to follow him. And Ryan has followed him to eternity."

Only a heart that has been embraced by God and Mama Mary can be brave and see the light.

A MOMENT WITH THE LORD

Lord, embrace me when I cannot find answers to my many questions in life. Amen.

A MOMENT WITH THE WORD

"Our Father in heaven, holy be your name, your kingdom come and your will be done…"

Matthew 6: 6-10

The big picture

This "*promdi*" (from the province) guy was in Manila for the first time. He was amazed at all the new sights and sounds, especially when he watched a basketball game at Araneta Coliseum. At halftime, spotting his townmate Pedro across the basketball court, he stood up and waved and shouted at the top of his voice, "Pedro! Pedro!" When someone lent him a pair of binoculars (larga vista), his voice dropped. "Pedro... Pedro," he said, almost in a whisper because Pedro looked so near!

A MOMENT WITH THE LORD

Lord, help me to see the big picture in everything that happens in my life. Help me to realize that there is a bigger world "out there", and there's always You "in here." Amen.

A MOMENT WITH THE WORD

"We do not fix our gaze on what is seen but on what is unseen."

2 Corinthians 4:18

A priest story

One day, a priest saw a beggar at the door of his church in Rome, and recognized that the beggar was his former classmate who had left the priesthood. Concerned about him, the priest told the story of his beggar-classmate to Pope John Paul II. A few days later, an invitation came from the Vatican for them to have a meal with the Pope. At the end of the meal, the Pope had a private talk with the beggar priest. What happened?

According to the story, the Holy Father asked him to hear his confession. When he protested that he was no longer a priest, the Holy Father looked at him with compassion and said: "Once a priest, always a priest." Close to tears, the beggar-priest asked that he be restored to his priestly faculties. After he heard the Pope's confession, he was appointed by the Pope to be the curate of the church where he had been begging with a special responsibility to attend to the beggars who seek alms at the church doors.

A MOMENT WITH THE LORD

Lord, remind me: "Once a priest, always a priest." Amen.

A MOMENT WITH THE WORD

"You are a priest forever according to the order of Melchizedek."

Hebrew 5:6

The dark stretch

As little children in Bani, Pangasinan, we looked forward to evenings when there was a program, a dance, or a movie in the town plaza. Going to the plaza was easy but going back home was a problem. We would have to pass a long, narrow, and unlighted stretch of road with a big mango tree that every child in town swore has a ghost in it. Gathering up all our courage, we would grab our rubber slippers and run as fast as we could, not looking back or to the side, but watching for the faint gate light up ahead and shouting at the top of our voices, "Papa, Mama, open the gate! Open the gate!"

A MOMENT WITH THE LORD

Lord, whenever I'm in a dark situation, give me a courageous and light heart. Let me not forget to focus on Your light and call on Your name. Amen.

A MOMENT WITH THE WORD

"Darkness is not dark for you, and night shines as the day."

Psalm 39:12

The dream house

Here's a story I heard about an architect who was retiring from a prestigious company. The president of the company asked him to build a dream house, an *obra maestra,* a showcase for his talent and know-how. Money was not to be a problem.

And so the architect started the project. But as he went on, he started skimping on the materials. Although the house looked beautiful on the outside, quality and safety were compromised. Finally, the house was finished. On the day of its inauguration, the president of the company announced that the house was to be the company's parting gift to the architect.

A MOMENT WITH THE LORD

Lord, help me to realize that when I fool others, it is myself that I fool. Amen.

A MOMENT WITH THE WORD

"But anyone who hears these words of mine and does not obey them is like a foolish man who built his house on sand. The rain poured down, the rivers flooded over, the wind blew hard against that house and it fell. And what a terrible fall that was!"

Matthew 7:6-7

From the mountaintop

Question: Why do mountain climbers rope themselves together?

Answer: To prevent the sensible ones from going home.

The Transfiguration was Jesus' way of "roping together" the disciples Peter, James and John with Himself. The experience of seeing His face shine like the sun, and His clothes become white as light, was for the disciples a peak experience that helped strengthen their belief in Him.

Was there a moment in your life when you experienced God in a very real and personal way? Our God is a God who reveals himself to us. He is not a God who is impersonal and indifferent. He is a God who goes the extra mile to seek us, and draw us closer to Him.

A MOMENT WITH THE LORD

Lord, in mountains high and valleys low, please be with me and be my guide. Amen.

A MOMENT WITH THE WORD

" *Cast all your cares to the Lord for he cares for you.*"
1 Peter 5:7

The handbrake

Any driver will tell you about feeling frustrated at not being able to get going despite stepping on the gas – and all because the handbrake is engaged.

Do you sometimes feel that life is a drag, and the journey is burdensome and difficult? Maybe it is because you haven't really "let go." Check your handbrake. Check it now!

A MOMENT WITH THE LORD

Lord, help me to let go of all those things that prevent me from going to You. Amen.

A MOMENT WITH THE WORD

"Trust God at all times, my people!"

Psalm 62:9

The radiator

In the course of my priestly duties, I do a lot of driving. One day, my eight-year-old car stopped dead and refused to restart. I found out that the radiator was empty of water and the engine had overheated and conked out.

Are you also running on empty? Are you drained out? Slow down. You might be overheating already. When that happens, you no longer radiate joy, peace, and love.

A MOMENT WITH THE LORD

Lord, help me to radiate love, peace and joy while I live. Help me to radiate Your warm presence wherever I go, whatever I do. Amen.

A MOMENT WITH THE WORD

"The fruit of the Spirit is love, joy, peace..."
                                                    Galatians 5:22

The spare tire

Faith is like a spare tire. We carry it with us everyday. In fact, we often take it for granted, even neglect or forget it, until we have a flat tire and we realize how lucky we are to have a spare tire. Like the spare tire that we should check to see if it is already flat or underinflated, faith must be constantly checked and, if necessary, inflated.

Faith, like the spare tire, can make the difference as we travel life's road. Take it along with you for it will give you the necessary strength. It is the key to a more confident travel.

A MOMENT WITH THE LORD

Lord, thank You so much for the gift of faith that has sustained me all these years. Amen.

A MOMENT WITH THE WORD

"Faith is the realization of what is hoped for and evidence of things not seen."

Hebrews 11:1

The Usher

The usher who meets us as we enter the dark movie house lights our way and leads us to our seats so that we can watch and enjoy the movie. The usher does not shine his light on himself. He points to something, someone greater than himself.

Are you self-effacing? Do you know how to be humble and fade away? Or are you so big that you are blocking the main event?

A MOMENT WITH THE LORD

Lord, let me be the one to lead the people to You, not to myself. Amen.

A MOMENT WITH THE WORD

"Teach me, O Lord, your way, lead me along a straight path."

Psalm 27:11

The value of a Mass

Going to Sunday Mass is not easy, especially when you are a little boy, and all you want to do is watch TV and play all day. I remember going to Mama one Sunday and telling her that I would just pray three rosaries at home instead of going to Sunday Mass. To this very day I cannot forget what she told me: "Jerry, not even 10, not even 20 rosaries can equal the value of one Mass."

A MOMENT WITH THE LORD

Lord, help me never to underestimate the value of every Mass. Amen.

A MOMENT WITH THE WORD

"Do this in memory of Me."

Luke 22:19b

Two visits

For many years it has been my habit to visit the Pink Sisters Adoration Convent whenever I go up to Baguio. Usually, I make one visit to the convent, but on this particular trip, there was a strong call for me to go back one more time, which I did. On my way out, I was followed by a man who introduced himself as a priest and who asked for the Sacrament of Reconciliation. It was a beautiful experience of faith, reconciliation and peace. As I was boarding my car, another man approached me and asked me for my blessing and absolution. He wanted to go back to the Church for he too had been away too long...

Now I know why the Lord called me to make two visits to the Pink Sisters' Convent in Baguio on that particular day.

A MOMENT WITH THE LORD

Lord, help me to be open and docile to the leading and prompting of Your spirit. Amen.

A MOMENT WITH THE WORD

"What man among you having a hundred sheep and losing one of them would not leave the ninety-nine in the desert and go after the lost one until he finds it?"

Luke 15:4

Vocation... *Bukasyon!*

"Father, do I have a vocation?" My answer to this question is a big resounding "YES!" We all have a vocation, a calling to be good, to be loving, and to be with the Lord in heaven. "Vocation" in Tagalog is *bukasyon*.

So be open (*maging bukas ka*) to whatever vocation God has chosen for you. And don't say, "*Bukas yun*" (Tomorrow) when God calls you; do not postpone your calling.

A MOMENT WITH THE LORD

Lord, help me to be sensitive and open to Your calling. Amen.

A MOMENT WITH THE WORD

"Oh, that today you would hear His voice, and harden not your hearts."

Hebrews 3:7-8

What 'sili' things can do

I remember a story told to us by our veteran missionary to Indonesia, Fr. Ben Prado, SVD. On one of his mission trips, his horse was going too slow and it was getting dark. He remembered that the natives had told him to put red pepper (sili) on the rear end of the horse to make it run faster. This he did, and the horse took off so fast it left him behind. Not knowing what to do, and not wanting to be left alone in the forest, he too put some sili on himself. He ran so fast that he caught up with his horse and even overtook it!

A MOMENT WITH THE LORD

Lord, help me to see humor and experience Your loving presence in all my undertakings. Amen.

A MOMENT WITH THE WORD

"A merry heart does good, like medicine."

Proverbs 17:22

Salve Regina

There is one song that would surely touch the heart of anyone who has been through the seminary – the "Salve Regina" or the "Hail Holy Queen" sung in Latin. It is the last song we sing before the lights are put off in the chapel. It is a song of love to Mama Mary, and a song of assurance.

I remember my first night in Christ the King Seminary. I was a boy of 12 then, so homesick and afraid, feeling lost and alone. Then I heard the song "Salve Regina." From that moment on, I just entrusted myself to Mama Mary. To this very day, I still remember feeling her loving embrace as the lights went off one by one, that first night in the seminary.

A MOMENT WITH THE LORD

Lord, thank you for giving us your Mother. I consecrate my life to her, and put myself under her special protection. Amen.

A MOMENT WITH THE WORD

"Hail Mary, full of grace the Lord is with you..."

Luke 1:28

A constant letting go

My cousin, Msgr. Marlo Peralta, parish priest of Pozorrubio, Pangasinan sent me this beautiful text message: "Notice how God opens millions of flowers every day without forcing the buds!"

Don't try to force anything. Let life be a constant letting go and letting God.

Maybe that's what living in God means, "a constant letting go, and letting God."

If you live in God, you will live well. If you live well, you will live on in the hearts of people, and you will live on with God in eternity.

A MOMENT WITH THE LORD

Lord, help me to live in You, so that I can live well, and live on. Amen.

A MOMENT WITH THE WORD

" I have the strength to face all conditions by the power that Christ gives me."

Philippians 4:13

A special penitent

A ll penitents are special.

But I have one special penitent. Papa Pio Luz is a special penitent because he says his confession to me in a special way. This 87- year-old man who uses a wheelchair, comes to our seminary with his driver. I would sit in the car's driver's seat while hearing his confession. After that, I would drive him around the seminary compound and we would have a joy-ride moment.

Now that's what I call a special service for a special penitent!

A MOMENT WITH THE LORD

Lord, remind me that every person is special, that every person is worth going out of my way for. Amen.

A MOMENT WITH THE WORD

"Yet I will rejoice in the Lord, and exalt in my saving God."

Habakkuk 3:8

An honest boy

One time while waiting for my car to be fixed, a little boy was pestering me to buy some cloth for cleaning the car. To dismiss him, I handed him 10 pesos for his efforts, but he refused, saying that his parents have taught him not to accept money that he did not work for. He said it with such dignity and sincerity.

What he did next was admirable. When he did not have change for the 100 pesos I gave him, he told me that he would leave all his stuff with me while he went to look for change. I told me that was not necessary, but he insisted, saying that he trusted me!

A MOMENT WITH THE LORD

Lord, bless and reward honest people who do not go for easy and dirty money. Amen.

A MOMENT WITH THE WORD

"If anyone is not willing to work, neither should that one eat."

2 Thessalonians 3:10

Mother and child

I have been to many funerals, but the saddest, by far, was that of a mother who died while giving birth to her child, and the child also died. The two were placed in the same coffin, together...

I could not imagine the pain of the husband whose marriage I officiated some nine months earlier. All he had and all that he ever dreamed of were gone.

I can never forget his words as I put my arms around him. "Father I cannot understand why.. but I will hold on, I will just hold on to God..."

A MOMENT WITH THE LORD

Lord, when I tend to magnify and amplify my pains, remind me that there are people around me who have bigger and more real pains. Amen.

A MOMENT WITH THE WORD

"Attend to my cry, for I am brought low indeed."
Psalm 142:6

Chosen brother

I have two brothers, *Manong* Oscar and Tim. But I have one more brother, the late Sonny Sison.

More than twenty years ago, Sonny told me. "Fr. Jerry, I have chosen you to become my brother. I want you to be my brother."

All these years, he had been a real brother to me. Aside from the hospitality and generosity he and his family had given me, I really appreciate his openness, honesty, and pieces of advice for my priesthood and ministry. As a brother, he was never lacking in giving me the support, the encouragement, and most of all, the respect I needed to go on.

I have chosen Sonny as my brother. He has gone ahead. But he will always be my chosen brother, "a special part of me, a special memory."

A MOMENT WITH THE LORD

Lord, thank you for choosing us to be your brothers and sisters inspite of our unworthiness. Amen.

A MOMENT WITH THE WORD

"Whoever does the will of the Father in heaven is for me brother, sister, or mother."

Matthew 12:50

Climbing trees

When was the last time you climbed a tree?

I remember how we, as children, climbed up trees to play, and pick its fruits. How beautiful to reminisce those days! But there were also times when we climbed a tree because a dog was chasing us, and the tree was our only refuge. We stayed up there captive, until the dog got tired barking and left us, or until someone rescued us.

As we grew older, we still climbed trees where no one can reach us, where we are safe, where we have control, or so we thought.

What is your tree of refuge?

Is it your money, your position, your pride? Is it your work, your vices, or your escapades?

Trees give us a lift, but they also limit us. You cannot stay up on a tree forever. Come down. Walk the earth. That's where the action is, with all its filth, sweat, and tears. But Jesus continues to walk with us. That's the greatest assurance. That's the only assurance. Come down!

A MOMENT WITH THE LORD

Lord, help me to come down from my tree of refuge and help me embrace the tree of the Cross. Amen.

A MOMENT WITH THE WORD

"Abba, all things are possible for you; take this cup away from me. Yet not what I want, but what you want."

Mark 14:36

Delicious apples

When we were growing up in the province, we saw and tasted apples only once a year, usually around Christmas time.

Any classmate who had an apple was an instant celebrity in the classroom. At that time, an apple was not to be eaten right away. It was something that was brought to school everyday to be shown off and to be flaunted, to be envied by others.

As children we flaunted apples. What do we flaunt to others now as grown-ups?

A MOMENT WITH THE LORD

Lord, help me never to make people feel their deprivations because they met me. Amen.

A MOMENT WITH THE WORD

"Those who are generous increase their riches; others are misers and impoverish themselves."

Proverbs 11:24

CR & CS

The comfort room (CR) and the convenience store (CS) are our most frequented, but often times, our most taken for granted places. Why? Well, that's because they are always there whenever we need them.

In life, too, there are people who are always there for us, but whom we take for granted. They are the CRs and CSs of our life.

Who are the people who are always there for you, and who are always at your beck and call, but often take for granted?

Remember them today. Don't abuse them. Respect them. Appreciate them.

Take time to thank them today.

Your CRs and CSs in life are your parents your helpers, your driver, your friend, your parish priest, and many more who have made life easier for you.

A MOMENT WITH THE LORD

Lord, help me to be aware, to be sensitive and to be grateful to many people who help me. Amen.

A MOMENT WITH THE WORD

"Clothe yourselves with humility in your dealings with one another."

1 Peter 5:5

First, last and only

Posted in the sacristy of our Mission House at Christ the King Seminary is this beautiful reminder:

"O PRIEST OF JESUS CHRIST, CELEBRATE THIS MASS AS IF IT WAS YOUR FIRST MASS, AS IF IT WAS YOUR LAST MASS, AS IF IT WAS YOUR ONLY MASS."

You, too, dear brother, dear sister: go, attend, and pray every Mass as if it was your first, your last, and your only Mass.

A MOMENT WITH THE LORD

Lord, help me to value, appreciate, and really treasure every Mass. Amen.

A MOMENT WITH THE WORD

"You are a chosen race, a community of priests, a consecrated nation, a people God has made His own to proclaim His wonders."

I Peter 2:9

For a day? Forever!

Wedding is only for a day.

Marriage is for a lifetime.

Someone rightly pointed out that the problem with many couples getting married is that they prepare well for their wedding, but not for their marriage..

Too focused on the icings and *borloloys*, they forget what is really essential in their life together.

Nowadays, some couples even hire an expensive wedding coordinator but forget to have a marriage Coordinator.

A MOMENT WITH THE LORD

Lord, help me not to focus on the icings and the trimmings, but on what is really important in life. Amen.

A MOMENT WITH THE WORD

"Man has to leave his father and mother, and be joined to his wife, and the two shall become one body."

Matthew 19:5

Giving light till the end

A story is told about two wounded soldiers who were recuperating in the same hospital room during World War II. Every day the soldier whose bed is beside the window would describe the outside world to the other soldier who lay in bed, paralyzed from the neck down. One morning, the soldier beside the window passed away.

That same morning, the paralyzed soldier found out that his friend who beautifully painted a scenery to him, making him want to get back on his feet, was blind, and that there was nothing outside the window but a wall.

Till the last moments of his life, the blind soldier who lived in darkness, gave light to someone.

A MOMENT WITH THE LORD

Lord, like a burning candle may I continue to give light and life to people around me who are in the dark. Amen.

A MOMENT WITH THE WORD

"You are the light of the world…"

Matthew 5:14

Forget me not?

"YOUR MOST IMPORTANT APPOINTMENT TODAY IS YOUR APPOINTMENT WITH THE HEAVENLY FATHER."

This text message I received recently made me realize how often I have set aside my prayer time because of my other seemingly more "pressing" and more "urgent" appointments.

Do you put off, leave out, or miss your appointment with God because you are so "busy doing God's work"?

A MOMENT WITH THE LORD

Lord, even if I forget you, please don't forget me. Amen.

A MOMENT WITH THE WORD

"Pride goes before destruction and haughtiness before a fall."

Proverbs 16:18

Front page

I wanted to leave a short but meaningful message to the rank and file of the Philippine National Police. It had to be simple. It had to be dramatic. So at the end of my pep talk, I unbuttoned my *polo barong,* exposing my T-shirt that had "I LOVE NYPD" printed on it. I told them how many Americans were proudly wearing them especially after the September 11 terrorist attack on World Trade Center. I ended my talk with a challenge and a hope that someday soon, Filipinos, too, will proudly wear "I LOVE PNP" T-shirts.

A Philippine Daily Inquirer reporter was there to cover the event, and there was a photo op. That's how my photo landed on the newspaper Philippine Daily Inquirer the next day.

A MOMENT WITH THE LORD

Lord, unworthy as I am, help me to spread your message simply and clearly. Amen.

A MOMENT WITH THE WORD

"Go and proclaim this message: The Kingdom of heaven is near."

Matthew 10:7

Birthday

The story is told about a man who looked sad on his birthday. When asked by a friend, he said: "It's my brother. He forgot my birthday last year, and he forgot again this year." "But that happens. Even brothers forget birthdays," the friend advised. "Even twin brothers?" the man sighed.

A MOMENT WITH THE LORD

Lord, help me to be thoughtful and considerate. Amen.

A MOMENT WITH THE WORD

"Let no kindness and fidelity leave you."

Proverbs 3:3

Goat magnate

My father was a lawyer, but he didn't have money. Maybe because he was a good man and didn't charge his poor clients. I remember how he helped many people from the barrios with their legal needs. He himself would do the typing in his old Underwood typewriter, and he would often ask me to get coffee for him and his clients.

On different occasions, the people he helped would give him rice, fruits, poultry or livestock as tokens of gratitude. One time, he received two goats which he wanted to be butchered because no one could take care of them. I pleaded that I will take care of them, which I did. I would gather grass, give them water, and let them out in the fields every afternoon after classes.

Soon the two goats multiplied, till I had about twelve, and felt like I was some goat magnate at the age of eight.

A MOMENT WITH THE LORD

Lord, help me to be grateful and faithful in little things. Amen.

A MOMENT WITH THE LORD

"It is better to be poor and honest than to be a fool and dishonest."

Proverbs 19:1

Guilt and shame

I still shudder with guilt and shame whenever I remember how we hunted birds with our slingshots when I was still a little boy. We knew where to hunt them and when to hunt them. The best time was whenever it rained. We took advantage of their helplessness when they were wet and cold, when they had to seek shelter in the trees. And we were there to pounce on them.

That was many years ago. I have grown up in the meantime. Sad to say, there are people who never grow up and continue to take advantage of the helplessness, the poverty, and the innocence of other people.

A MOMENT WITH THE LORD

Lord, forgive me for the times I used, abused and took advantage of the less fortunate. Amen.

A MOMENT WITH THE WORD

"If any of you should cause one of these little ones...to stumble and fall, it would be better for you to be thrown into the depths of the sea..."

Matthew 18:6

Our Lady of Medugorje

Holy cow

I heard this story from our Irish confrere Fr. John O'Mahony: A Mother Superior of a small congregation in a remote village was dying and she would not eat or would not even drink milk. One of the nuns saw an Irish whiskey in the kitchen, and poured a generous amount into a glass of milk. When the Mother Superior tasted it, she took one sip, and then one more, till she finished the whole glass!

After she said her goodbye and gave her last minute instructions, she closed her eyes. Suddenly, she opened them again and uttered: "Oh, one more thing, no matter what happens to our congregation, don't sell that cow!"

And she expired, with a smile.

A MOMENT WITH THE LORD

Lord, help me to see the humor, the surprise, and the twist, even in the most difficult situations. Amen.

A MOMENT WITH THE WORD

"Serve the Lord with gladness, come before Him with joyful song."

Psalm 100:2

Honesto and Prudentio

During a four-hour flight from Los Angeles to Manila, when the cabin lights were already dimmed, a PAL steward approached me. He found a set of dentures in one of the lavatories. He wanted to find the owner of the dentures, but on the other hand, he did not want to embarrass the owner by announcing it publicly.

So he went around approaching every passenger, asking discreetly who the owner was.

I commended him for his sense of propriety and sensitivity. As I saw him move on, I smiled and said to myself, I just met an honest and a prudent steward.

A MOMENT WITH THE LORD

Lord, help me to be your honest, helpful, and prudent steward in this life. Amen.

A MOMENT WITH THE WORD

"Whoever can be trusted in little things can also be trusted in great ones, whoever is dishonest in slight matters will also be dishonest in greater ones."

Luke 16:10

Impressive

Some people are really impressive. You take a look at them and they have impressive looks, impressive bank accounts, impressive achievements, impressive social standing, impressive background, and impressive bearings.

Wow!

I wish though that they were more expressive.

A MOMENT WITH THE LORD

Lord, help me to live not so much an impressive but an expressive life. Amen.

A MOMENT WITH THE WORD

"God resists the proud but bestows His favor on the lowly."

James 4:6

Is that you?

Did you hear the story about a man who died and was praised to high heavens during the funeral Mass? Feeling uncomfortable, the widow was overheard whispering to her son: "Will you please go and look in the coffin and check if it's your Dad!"

A MOMENT WITH THE LORD

Lord, remind me that I may get away with it sometime, but not all the time, especially at the last time. Amen.

A MOMENT WITH THE WORD

"Do not consider yourself wise, fear God, and turn away from evil."

Proverbs 3:7

Keep digging

Did you hear about the two-seater plane that crashed on a snow-covered cemetery somewhere in Europe?

According to the latest report, 50 bodies have already been dug up, and the digging goes on!

A MOMENT WITH THE LORD

Lord, help me not to be afraid to continue digging in my search for a truthful and meaningful life. Amen.

A MOMENT WITH THE LORD

"There is nothing covered that will not be uncovered, and nothing hidden that will not be made known. What I am telling you in the dark, you must speak in the light. What you hear in private, proclaim from the housetops."

Matthew 10:26-27

Laugh more often

I was feeling tired and low when I received this text message that really made me laugh.

"NEVER, UNDER ANY CIRCUMSTANCES, TAKE A SLEEPING PILL AND LAXATIVE ON THE SAME NIGHT!"

When was the last time you really had a good laugh?

I read somewhere that children laugh an average of 400 ha! ha! ha's a day while we adults only laugh 20 ha! ha! ha's, if we do at all.

Laughter is good for the heart and for the soul. Lough more often. Laugh now!

A MOMENT WITH THE LORD

Lord, thank you for the gift of laughter. Help me to use it more often. Amen.

A MOMENT WITH THE WORD

"Enjoy happiness and do not reject lawful pleasure when it comes your way."

Sirach 14:14

Learn from the geese

During one of our council meetings, Fr. Joel Maribao, former Provincial Superior of the SVD Philippine Central Province, shared this beautiful story about the geese, and his reflections:

The geese, as a flock, can fly 71% farther than if each goose flew alone.

When the leader of the flock gets tired, he will go back to the rear of the V-formation to allow another goose to take his place.

The geese in the rear position "honk" to encourage and give a boost to those in front.

When one of the geese gets sick or wounded, and falls out of formation, two geese will follow it on its flight downwards to protect it.

A MOMENT WITH THE LORD

Teach us, Lord, not to fly alone, that we can fly higher if we are together. Lord, teach us to encourage, and affirm each other, to minister to one another, and suffer vicariously for one another. Amen.

A MOMENT WITH THE WORD

"So that they may all be one, as you, Father, are in me…"

John 17:21

I am Here

I would like to share with you a song which I composed after my first pilgrimage to Guadalupe, Mexico. I was driving alone on a lonely road one evening on my way to Pangasinan, when the music and the lyrics of this song just came to life.

I AM HERE, I'M YOUR MOTHER
DO NOT FEAR, I AM NEAR!

I am with you when you wake up in the morning
Through the whole day, till evening comes again;

I am with you in your work and undertakings,
In your journeys, in your joys and in your songs!

There'll be problems, there'll be pain and persecutions
There'll be trials, but be joyful and be strong!

When in danger, call my name and I'll come running
If you fall down, hold my hand I'll help you stand.

A MOMENT WITH THE LORD

Lord, thank you for giving me your Mother who is always near. Amen.

A MOMENT WITH THE WORD

"Behold your Mother."

John 19:27

Mama's boy

Yes, I am a Mama's boy.

I am my Mama's boy, and I am Mama Mary's boy. My own experiences and feelings towards my Mama are my experiences and feelings towards Mama Mary.

I relate to Mama Mary not so much from the biblical, theological or dogmatic point of view. I relate to her as a son, more rightly, as a sinful, desperate son who clings to her no matter what. It's just that I believe she is my mother, and that she will help me, she will not let go of me, she will make exceptions for me and she will make all things beautiful in God's sweet time.

Presumptuous? Maybe. But, it is better to be presumptuous of the Lord's and Mama Mary's love than to doubt. It is better to believe that those we love, love us too.

A MOMENT WITH THE LORD

Lord, thank You for giving me a loving mother in Mama, and in Mama Mary. Amen.

A MOMENT WITH THE WORD

"Can a mother forget her infant, be without tenderness for the child of her womb?"

Isaiah 49:15

Humor and sacrifice

The story is told about a young man who walked over to the table of an elderly couple and said: "Lolo, I can't help but be inspired and be edified. I saw you buy a burger; give half of it to your wife, and you just kept looking at her while she ate."

The old man looked at him and replied: "Oh, that. You see we have only one set of dentures. I had to wait for her to finish her half."

A MOMENT WITH THE LORD

Lord, remind me that true love requires lots of patience, humor, and sacrifice. Amen.

A MOMENT WITH THE WORD

"Love is patient and kind..."

1 Corinthians 13:4

Monkey business?

I gave a banana to my pet monkey, Milenio today, and you know what he did? He grabbed the fruit, climbed the tree as fast as he could to get away from me, and from up there, he sneered and jeered at me while he hurriedly and voraciously consumed his banana.

I gave him a banana the next day, and he did exactly the same thing. I'll give him a banana again tomorrow, and he'll probably do the same thing. I guess I'll keep on giving a banana to this ungrateful creature...

After all, he is a monkey and acts like a monkey. But, there are people who are selfish and ungrateful, like the monkey.

A MOMENT WITH THE LORD

Lord, forgive me when I get involved in monkey business i.e. busy-ness in grabbing, with no sharing and with no thanksgiving... Amen.

A MOMENT WITH THE WORD

"So you shall not wrong one another but you shall fear your God..."

Leviticus 25:17

My favorite jacket

When I was in Grade I, Mama gave me a hand-me-down jacket which came from my cousins in Manila. I really loved the jacket. It was a red and blue reversible jacket made of fine corduroy. Every time I wore it, it gave me that *guwapo*, smart and cowboy feeling. It earned me some *pogi* points.

Then, one early morning, a fire broke out in our neighborhood leaving many homeless. Mama said we should give something to the fire victims. I still don't know how it happened but I ended up giving my treasured jacket to my classmate who was one of the victims.

I have had many jackets since then, but I still remember my red and blue reversible corduroy jacket, the one that I loved, the one that I gave away.

A MOMENT WITH THE LORD

Lord, help me to give, till it really hurts. Amen.

A MOMENT WITH THE WORD

"Let them do good, be rich in good deeds and be generous; let them share with others."

I Timothy 6:18

Never enough

It was about 11 p.m. when my cell phone rang. It was a call from Efren, an ex-seminarian (XVD), who sounded so distraught. He just arrived home, found his 75-year-old mother lying dead on her bed.

In no time at all, the XVDs came to his assistance because Efren didn't know what to do.

When I came to see Efren, I pointed out his sacrifice, his love, his devotion to his mother. It was at this point when Efren broke down and cried, muttering, "*Kulang pa*, Father, *Kulang pa*!" (It was not enough, Father, it was not enough!)

Yes, we can never love enough. We can never love too much.

A MOMENT WITH THE LORD

Lord, help me never to say "Enough!" when it comes to love. Amen.

A MOMENT WITH THE LORD

"Don't get tired of doing what is good."
2 Corinthians 4:9

Pray on

Have you ever prayed so hard and pleaded to God with all your heart?

In 1987, when my father was in the ICU fighting for his life, I really burned the lines to heaven with prayers. All I was asking from God was to give Papa some more years to live. After all, he was such a good man. Besides, I was His priest serving Him. Why could He not give me this one special favor?

I bargained with God. I pleaded, offered sacrifices and good works, did everything, just for my Papa to get well.

God did not answer my prayer, but what is important is that I knew there was someone to pray to, and that, in itself, is the value of prayer.

A MOMENT WITH THE LORD

Lord, even when I don't get what I'm asking for, thanks anyway, for being there for me. Amen.

A MOMENT WITH THE WORD

"At every opportunity, pray in the Spirit, using prayers and petitions of every sort. Pray constantly and attentively..."
Ephesians 6:18

Stay in peace

Think about it: "If people talk behind your back, it simply means that you are two steps ahead of them."

A MOMENT WITH THE LORD

Lord, help me to stay in peace, no matter what, no matter where. Amen.

A MOMENT WITH THE WORD

" And may the peace of Christ reign in your hearts, because it is for this that you were called together in one body."

Colossians 3:15

Stay on course

I was driving home alone on my way to Pangasinan, negotiating the North expressway at about 90 kph. All of a sudden, I found myself enveloped in a thick and heavy smoke caused by grass fire. For the next few seconds (which seemed like eternity), there was nothing I could see up ahead. It was as if time stood still. All I could do was to slow down and pray. I also made sure that I stayed on my lane and did not change course.

I guess it's the same in life: When you are not sure where you are going, slow down, pray, and stay on course.

A MOMENT WITH THE LORD

Lord, guide me, lead me, stay with me as I travel life's road. Amen.

A MOMENT WITH THE WORD

"Teach me, O Lord, your way; lead me along a straight path."

Psalm 27:11

The acacia tree

There used to stand outside my room a tall acacia tree. It was often the subject of conversation and admiration of many passers-by because of its wide branches and lofty stature. But two years ago, a powerful typhoon felled this once proud tree to the ground. Why? Because it was not deeply rooted. It had height but not depth. That which was once tall and proud was shamed and humbled.

A MOMENT WITH THE LORD

Lord, remind me that it is the humble who shall inherit the earth. Amen.

A MOMENT WITH THE WORD

"Whoever exalts himself shall be humbled, but whoever humbles himself shall be exalted."

Matthew 23:12

The conductor

Do you know what I wanted to become when I was a little boy? I wanted to become a bus conductor. At that time, the Pantranco buses were open on one side, and I admired how the bus conductor would go from the rear to the front and vice versa, giving out tickets, collecting fares, hanging on to the open side while the bus was in motion. He is also the guy helping the passengers with their pieces of luggage. The driver did the driving, but it was the conductor who did all the serving.

Little did I know that I would become some kind of a "conductor" someday – a priest who conducts people to God and vice versa, and a person who does a lot of serving.

A MOMENT WITH THE LORD

Lord, while I live, let me be your conductor, by serving you and your people. Amen.

A MOMENT WITH THE WORD

"Be like the Son of Man who has come, not to be served but to serve and to give His life to redeem many."
Matthew 20:28

Upset? Angry?

Do you easily get upset by people, things or events around you? Don't! Remember, when you get UPSET, you have been SETUP by the evil one.

Do you get angry easily? Don't! Remember, when you get angry, you punish yourself unnecessarily.

Should you get upset or angry, remember the wet cement: the longer you stay on it, the harder it will be to get out of it.

A MOMENT WITH THE LORD

Lord, help me not to allow anything or anyone to upset me or make me angry. Amen.

A MOMENT WITH THE WORD

"The hotheaded one provokes disputes, while the one slow to anger reconciles differences."

Proverbs 15:18

What's your song?

If Mass songs were to be the theme songs of married couples at different stages of their married life, it will go this way:

Newly married couples will sing the joyful *Papuri sa Diyos!* (i.e Gloria in Excelsis Deo! Glory to God in the Highest!)

After one year of marriage the couple starts singing the remorseful *Panginoon Maawa ka* (i.e Kyrie or Lord Have Mercy).

After some years of marriage, some couples are singing desperately *Kunin Mo, O Diyos at Tanggapin Mo!* (i.e Take Lord and Receive!).

Married couples, what song are you singing now?

A MOMENT WITH THE LORD

Lord, through the years, may I never stop singing gratefully your praises and your glory. Amen.

A MOMENT WITH THE WORD

"So I will sing praises to your name and fulfill my vows day after day."

Psalm 61:9

Simple joys

As a little boy growing up in Bani, Pangasinan, I didn't experience the thrill of playing video games or owning any high-tech toys. We didn't have electricity but we had our imagination, and we had Mother Nature. We had simple moments. Simple joys.

I memorized every kind of tree in our backyard, and I knew every nook and corner. When a particular fruit is in season, I knew which tree to visit. I remember how my friends and I would hide the fruits not yet ripe for picking, with branches and leaves, and prayed that other boys would not discover our "precious treasure."

A MOMENT WITH THE LORD

Lord, among my many treasures in life, let me not lose sight of my real treasure. Amen.

A MOMENT WITH THE WORD

"Do not store up treasure for yourself here on earth... Store up treasure for yourself with God."

Matthew 6:19

Zip-lock plastic bag

You may have seen one.
   You may even have one.
But don't be one: a zip-lock plastic bag.

   Don't be one who zips other people up.
   Don't be one who is so locked up.
   Don't be plastic.

A MOMENT WITH THE LORD

   Lord, help me not to become a zip-lock plastic bag as I go through life. Amen.

A MOMENT WITH THE WORD

   "...for they do not do as they say. They tie up heavy burdens and load them on the shoulders of the people, but they do not even raise a finger to move them."
                                                      Matthew 23:4

Me first?

Someone observed that in pre-war Iraq, the women always walked behind their husbands. After the war, the men started walking behind the women. A Western reporter asked an Iraqi man why. Was it because of some kind of a conversion, or a realization about a women's rights? The Iraqi man's response? Land mines!

A MOMENT WITH THE LORD

Lord, help me to be, and to remain, a person, even in a crowd. Amen.

A MOMENT WITH THE WORD

"Whoever wants to be first must place himself last of all and be the servant of all."

Mark 9:3

A lesson from the rice stalks

One day, I was walking with an old farmer-guide during one of my village mission trips in Abra. As we passed by the rice fields, I pointed at the tall rice stalks that swayed in the wind. I told the farmer how bountiful the harvest would be that year.

The farmer, without even looking at the rice talks, taught me a lesson I could never forget. "Father," he said, "those rice stalks that stand tall and straight are empty and have nothing. It is those which are bent and lowly that are heavy with grain..."

A MOMENT WITH THE LORD

Lord, help me to remain good and humble, and not to envy those who seem to prosper by evil ways. Amen.

A MOMENT WITH THE WORD

"God resists the proud but bestows His favor on the lowly."

James 4:6

Amazing

Remember the story about a boy who was named "Amazing" by his father? He became the butt of jokes because of his name, so much so that he asked that his name be not inscribed in his tombstone so that people would forget his name forever.

And so on his tombstone were written just the date of birth, and the date of death, no name. But whenever people saw this, they always ended up saying, "that's amazing!"

A MOMENT WITH THE LORD

Lord, never mind the amazing things. Just help me leave behind a good name. Amen.

A MOMENT WITH THE WORD

"I can never forget you! I have written your name in the palm of my hands."

Isaiah 49:16

And counting...

Teacher:	What comes after the number 8?
Boy:	Number 9 Ma'am.
Teacher:	What comes after the number 9?
Boy:	Number 10 Ma'am.
Teacher:	Wow! Who taught you how to count?
Boy:	My father Ma'am.
Teacher:	Okay, what comes after the number 10?
Boy:	Jack Ma'am, then Queen, then King!

A MOMENT WITH THE LORD

Lord, help me to give good examples to those around me. Amen.

A MOMENT WITH THE WORD

"I beg you, then, to follow my example."

1 Corinthians 4:16

Christian ?

The story is told about a small boy who sat with his mother in church. During the homily, the priest kept asking the question "What is a Christian?" each time pounding his fist on the pulpit.

Feeling nervous with the repeated questioning, the little boy whispered to his mother, "Mama, do you know what a Christian is?"

"Yes, dear, just sit and listen," said the mother. When the priest thundered again "What is a Christian?" this time pounding extra hard on the pulpit, the nervous boy jumped and cried: "Tell him Mama! Tell him!"

A MOMENT WITH THE LORD

Lord, help me to live my life in such a way that others will know You and see Your face.   Amen.

A MOMENT WITH THE WORD

" If we walk in the light as he is in the light, we have fellowship with one another."

John 1:7

Are you ready?

I always carry with me in my car the oil for the anointing of the sick, in case of emergency. I cannot count now the times in the past when I stopped to bless and anoint people, especially those involved in accidents.

One day, while driving through Aurora Boulevard, Cubao, I stopped to anoint two alleged hold-up men who were just gunned down by the police. It was not only a stomach-churning but also a heart-breaking moment to see how life has become so cheap these days.

Indeed, we do not know the time nor the hour.

A MOMENT WITH THE LORD

Lord, help me to live in such a way that I will be ready wherever and whenever. Amen.

A MOMENT WITH THE WORD

"Prepare to meet your God."

Amos 4:12

Called by name

The story is told about a mother who named all his six sons Joselito. When asked how her children get to know whom she is calling, her response was: "Oh, that's easy. I call them by their family names."

A MOMENT WITH THE LORD

Thank you, Lord, for you know me not only by my name, but by heart. Amen.

A MOMENT WITH THE WORD

"I have called you by name."

Isaiah 43:1

'Canonized'

My brother *Manong* Oscar was one of those hit by a water canon at the Mendiola bridge by the police last Oct. 14, 2005. When I met him after that incident, I said to him: "Congratulations, *Manong*! You are the first member of our family to be 'canonized'"!

It was my way of saying I admired him for his convictions and my being one with him in that humbling experience for the sake of service to our people.

A MOMENT WITH THE LORD

Lord, remind me that I am blessed whenever people persecute me because of truth and because of You. Amen.

A MOMENT WITH THE WORD

"Happy are you when people insult you and persecute you and tell all kinds of evil lies against you because you are my followers."

Matthew 5:11

October

**Our Lady of Manaoag
Our Lady of the
Most Holy Rosary**

Delivery room moment

It was a rare privilege to be right there in the delivery room where I was born. After celebrating Mass at the San Carlos General Hospital in Bolingit, Pangasinan, I asked the head nurse where the old delivery room of the hospital was, and she gladly brought me to the place.

In the middle of the room, there was the old delivery table. I said a prayer for my Mama who suffered so much when she gave birth to me (she told me so at my ordination!) and for Papa, too, who must have worried much and prayed hard outside that delivery room on October 1, 1953...

A MOMENT WITH THE LORD

Lord, You were there even before I was born. Grant that I may accomplish whatever mission You have for me in life. Amen.

A MOMENT WITH THE WORD

"You are mine. Before I formed you, I knew you. And before you were born, I consecrated you."

Jeremiah 1:5

Angel moment

Take a moment and acknowledge the presence of your Guardian Angel. God, in His thoughtfulness, has assigned to each one of us a personal "bodyguard" to protect and defend us. Those slips, those near-misses, those unexplainable decisions or sudden stops – can you not see someone shielding and guiding you through it all?

Your Guardian Angel is not only a "bodyguard" but also a "soulguard" as well! He whispers, "Do good, be good," against the devil's "Do bad, be bad." Your Guardian Angel rejoices when you do good, and becomes sad when you do bad.

Your Guardian Angel can be anywhere you are. He is always there just like a good, reliable friend.

A MOMENT WITH THE LORD

"Angel of God, my guardian dear, to whom God's love commits me here. Ever this day, be at my side, to light and guard, to rule and guide. Amen."

A MOMENT WITH THE WORD

"For to his angels he has given command about you, that they guard you in all your ways."

Psalm 91:11

A mother's heart

After one year in Our Lady of Guadalupe Seminary, my brother *Manong* Oscar decided that the priesthood was not for him. He was already late for enrollment. In fact classes had started already, but Mama pleaded, did not give up and asked that she be given a chance to talk to Fr. Chicote, OAR, then the principal of San Sebastian College. Father Chicote relates to this very day that when he saw my brother's good grades and my Mama's crying heart, right away, he accommodated *Manong* to the last section of the second year high school. My brother graduated 3 years later as valedictorian of the class... because of one person who understood and because of a mother who did not give up.

A MOMENT WITH THE LORD

Lord, give me an understanding heart, a persevering heart. Amen.

A MOMENT WITH THE WORD

"Let us not grow weary while doing good, for in due season we shall reap if we do not lose heart."

Galatians 6:9

Coincidence

A teacher asked his class to give an example of "coincidence." There was a long silence. Then, a small boy raised his hands and said: "My father and mother were married on the same day!"

Was it a coincidence that you married each other? Was it an accident? But then, nothing happens by accident for those who love God. Was it destiny? Or maybe magic? Didn't the song say, "Could it be magic? For how can two people in a world so full of strangers find each other?" Whatever. There was a reason why you married each other. There is a mission why you are still married and should stay married, together.

A MOMENT WITH THE LORD

Lord, remind me that because of you, there are no accidents or coincidences in this life. Amen.

A MOMENT WITH THE WORD

"You, Lord are all I have, and you give me all I need; my future is in your hands."

Psalm 16:5

Dealing with pain

The story is told about a patient who was writhing in pain, and so he asked his doctor's help. After some thought, the doctor said: "OK, I'll give you morphine".

In response, the patient cried out: "No, doctor, I want less pain, not more pain!"

A MOMENT WITH THE LORD

Lord, help me deal with pain, and not to escape in vain. Amen.

A MOMENT WITH THE WORD

"Those who do not take up their cross and follow in my steps are not fit to be my disciples."

Matthew 10:38

Gentleness of soul

Someone once said that if religion has done nothing to your temper, then it has not done much to your soul.

Why is it that there are people who claim to love God, yet go on hurting other people?

Why is it that there are people who have so many devotions and are prayerful, but are proud, arrogant, and deceitful?

Before you talk about your religion or your devotions, let's talk first about gentleness of your soul.

A MOMENT WITH THE LORD

Lord, teach me humility and gentleness of soul. Amen.

A MOMENT WITH THE WORD
"But the Spirit produces love, joy, peace, patience, kindness, goodness, faithfulness, humility, and self-control."
Galatians 5:22

Rosary moment

Take some time to look at the rosary. It is made up of a lot of beads, right? Remember the story of the missionary who taught a convert how to pray the rosary, but was surprised why he finished the rosary very fast? The convert explained, "Well, I prayed one Hail Mary, and then I said, 'the same, the same, the same, the same, *pareho, pareho lang, pareho pa rin!*'"

And did you know that our guardian angels carry a rose to the feet of the Blessed Mother with every Hail Mary we pray? So next time you are tempted to rush the rosary, please think of your poor guardian angel, tired and harrassed from going back and forth at top speed!

A MOMENT WITH THE LORD

Lord, teach me to pray not just with my lips, but with a sincere heart. Amen.

A MOMENT WITH THE WORD

"At every opportunity pray in the spirit, using prayers and petitions of every sort. Pray constantly and attentively for all in the holy company."

Ephesians 6:18

Walk with God

It happenes every time we have our pilgrimages on foot from Urdaneta to Manaoag, a Marian shrine in Pangasinan. I had many "Walk with God" moments, a walk which I started in October 1989 for thanksgiving and petitions.

Along the 13-kilometer way, we would pray the rosary continuously, and I would hear confessions while walking. Some penitents would walk by my side asking for my absolution and blessing while sharing with me their umbrella to shield me. It is indeed a beautiful picture of collaboration between the clergy and the laity... all pilgrims on our way to the Father!

A MOMENT WITH THE LORD

Lord, stay with us and help us to hold on to You and to one another on our way to the Father. Amen.

A MOMENT WITH THE WORD

"You should be like one, big, happy family, full of sympathy toward each other, loving one another with tender hearts and humble minds."

1 Peter 3:8

Group picture moment

I experienced one cathartic moment recently during a group picture-taking.

We were all set with our beautiful (automatic!) smile when one from the group shouted "stop!", and went to break a branch from a poor, frail, fragile plant that was "blocking the view."

Upon reflection, I realized how many of us break people's hopes and dreams just to be in the picture. The poor plant's only fault was that it was there all these years trying to survive, and we came in just for a 5-minute photo opportunity, and killed it.

May all of us, especially our leaders, realize that we are all just passing by. May we not in any way destroy the people, the values, and the institutions that have been there before us and will be there long after we are gone.

A MOMENT WITH THE LORD

Lord, help me not to break people's hopes and dreams. Amen.

A MOMENT WITH THE WORD

"Love one another with mutual affection; anticipate one another in showing honor."

Romans 12:10

Missionaries by design

You out there, you who live abroad, think about it. Has it ever occurred to you that you are where you are now because God wanted you to be there? Maybe you left the country for financial or family reasons, but have you ever considered that you are where you are now because of God's plan? Nothing happens by accident for those who love God. You are where you are now because God has a mission for you to do there.

A MOMENT WITH THE LORD

Lord, help me to realize that I am a missionary wherever I go, whatever I do. Amen.

A MOMENT WITH THE WORD

"Go to the whole world and preach the gospel to all nations."

Mark 16:15

For love

Marlon and Matet were set to be wed one October evening at San Agustin Church, but the heavy downpour had caused tremendous traffic all over Metro Manila. When it became apparent that the traffic was not going to ease up, Marlon alighted from his car and walked for one hour from Dapitan to the church, in his *barong* and new shoes – all because Matet was already waiting for him. What a beautiful love story about a man who walked with love in his heart, and a woman who waited with patience for his love!

A MOMENT WITH THE LORD

Lord, nothing is heavy if the heart is light, nothing is difficult if there is love. Amen.

A MOMENT WITH THE WORD

"There is no limit to love's forbearance, to its trust, its hope, its power to endure."

1 Corinthians 13:7

Humility

Fr. Raymond Soriano, SVD, my classmate who is now assigned in Australia writes about this story:

A lawyer, driving on a country road, encountered a crowd in one intersection. Thinking cleverly and wanting to throw his weight around to get to the scene, he shouted, "Let me through! I am a relative of the victim!" Upon hearing this, the crowd made way for him and lo and behold, lying in front of everyone was a dead pig run over by a car.

A MOMENT WITH THE LORD

Lord, help me to remember that the way to find you is not through deceit and pride but through honesty and humility. Amen.

A MOMENT WITH THE WORD

"Clothe yourselves with humility in your dealings with one another."

I Peter 5:5

In control

I saw this beautiful advertisement at the back of a bus with this message: "Next time, relax, take the bus, and leave the driving to us."

Time was when I insisted to do all the driving myself. I always wanted to be in control, and I didn't want anybody to drive for me. But now, honestly, I'm happy if others can drive for me. I have come to accept that I need people to help bring me to my destination.

A MOMENT WITH THE LORD

Lord, teach me to let go and to let you and others do the driving. Amen.

A MOMENT WITH THE WORD

"I place myself in your care. You will save me, Lord; you are a faithful God."

Psalm 31:5

Inferiority complex

Did you hear the story about a man who had such a strong inferiority complex? He was so shy that whenever he entered an elevator and gave the attendant his floor number, he always meekly added, "If it isn't out of your way."

A MOMENT WITH THE LORD

Lord, help me to learn how to go out of my way for others, like you. Amen.

A MOMENT WITH THE WORD

"He must become more important while I become less important."

John 3:30

In your eyes

I read somewhere recently that one out of three persons is ugly. So, if you look at the person on your left and he or she is handsome or beautiful, *delicado ka na.* (You're in a precarious situation) If you look at the person on your right and he or she is handsome or beautiful, *may problema ka na!* (You have a problem)

A MOMENT WITH THE LORD

Lord, remind me that everyone is beautiful in your eyes. Amen.

A MOMENT WITH THE WORD

"And before you were born, I consecrated you."
Jeremiah 1:5

JP II

Were not our hearts burning?

This phrase best describes every encounter with Pope John Paul II. A lot has been said and will still be said about our beloved Pope JP II, but what best describes him is that he was a man who prayed much. He drew strength from prayers. He spent at least 3 hours before the Blessed Sacrament every day. To us, he was a Pope, but to God, he was a vicar servant, and to the Blessed Mother, he was a son. It was prayer that made him constantly aware of who he was and what he should be. He humbled himself before God in prayer, that's why he was able to bring God everywhere.

A MOMENT WITH THE LORD

Lord, without prayer, I'm just a player, and I am just a pretender. Amen.

A MOMENT WITH THE WORD

"Then you will call to me. You will come and pray to me, and I will answer you. You will seek me, and you will find me because you will seek me with all your heart."

Jeremiah 29:12-13

Just passing by

received this text message which is really worth pondering upon: "Strange how people can be so pre-occupied with a life they can't hold on to, and neglect an eternity they can't run away from."

Yes, time is passing. Eternity is waiting.

A MOMENT WITH THE LORD

Lord, remind me that what matters most in the end is the love I carried in my heart, and the love I have shared in my life. Amen.

A MOMENT WITH THE WORD

"Teach us how short our life is, so that we may become wise."

Psalm 90:12

Know why ?

The story is told about a guru who ordered the Ashram cat to be tied during the evening worship so as not to disturb the worshippers. After the guru died, the cat continued to be tied, and when the cat died, another cat was brought to the Ashram so that it could be tied during the evening worship.

And so it was that years and years later, many treatises were written by the guru's scholarly disciples on the liturgical significance of tying up a cat during worship.

A MOMENT WITH THE LORD

Lord, help me to stay focused and stick to the essentials as I go through life. Amen.

A MOMENT WITH THE WORD

"Instead, be holy in all that you do, just as God who called you is holy."

1 Peter 1:15

More power

The story is told about a priest who accompanied a convict to the electric chair. What was he to say to console a man about to die? "Goodbye"? "Take care"? "See you later"? All these seemed inappropriate, and he became desperate for the right words to say.

Finally, as the convict got to the electric chair, the priest patted the man on the head and said, "More power to you!"

A MOMENT WITH THE LORD

Lord, may my words be a source of comfort to others. Amen.

A MOMENT WITH THE WORD

"As a mother comforts her son, so will I comfort you..."
Isaiah 66:13

Leaning

According to a text message I received, it is not true that beer makes you fat. On the contrary, beer makes you lean – lean on walls, lean on doors, and lean on people.

A MOMENT WITH THE LORD

Lord, help me to lean on you alone. Amen.

A MOMENT WITH THE WORD

"Trust in the Lord with all your heart and lean not on your own understanding."

Proverbs 3:5

Missing the point

There is a story about a hunter who discovered that his new dog could walk on water. Overjoyed, he invited his neighbor to go with him the following day. Sure enough the dog would walk on water to retrieve every duck they hit. Unable to contain his excitement, the hunter blurted out: "Did you notice anything unusual about my dog?"

After some thought, the neighbor replied: "Yeah, your dog can't swim."

A MOMENT WITH THE LORD

Lord, teach me to see your blessings and miracles in my life. Amen.

A MOMENT WITH THE WORD

"So then, as the Holy Spirit says, if you hear God's voice today, do not be stubborn..."

Hebrews 3:7

Money, money

Fatima Soriano, who has inspired so many people by her simplicity and joy, told me that she dreamt of Mama Mary who pointed to her some money. But as the money increased it suddenly became dark, she said.

Yes, money can brighten up your life, but too much money can actually darken it.

A MOMENT WITH THE LORD

Lord, remind me that the lights go out when money becomes my God. Amen.

A MOMENT WITH THE WORD

"Have nothing to do with the worthless things that people do, things that belong to the darkness, instead bring them out of the light."

Ephesians 5:11

Last request

There is a story about a priest who asked the convict seated at the electric chair if he had a last request. "Yes, Father. Please stay with me and hold my hands," was the convict's reply.

A MOMENT WITH THE LORD

Lord, remind me that you will be with me no matter what. Amen.

A MOMENT WITH THE WORD

"I will always be with you; I will never abandon you."
Joshua 1:5

P 100 bill

Remember the story about a guy who found P100 on the road? He picked it up with much joy, and the story could have ended there on a happy note.

But you know what happened? From then on, whenever he walked, his eyes would be focused on the road hoping to find another P100 bill. And so it happened that after many years of walking with his back bent and his eyes focused on the ground, he became a hunchback. He didn't even care to see the sunset and he hardly looked at people's faces, all because he kept looking for more P100 bills.

Worse, he even forgot to look up to his God because he kept looking for more P100 bills.

A MOMENT WITH THE LORD

Lord, remind me that there are more important things in life than money. Amen.

A MOMENT WITH THE WORD

"Instead, be concerned above everything else with the Kingdom of God and with what he requires of you, and he will provide you with all these other things."

Matthew 6:33

My ordination prayer

When a man finally reaches the altar of the Lord, he literally has come a long way. It took me 16 years from first year high school till ordination, and all those formative years have taught me to be grateful to God who is faithful and merciful. I have been called and chosen in spite of my sins and weaknesses... in spite of my unworthiness. I find consolation in the thought that God uses not so much the worthy instrument but the willing instrument.

Below is my ordination prayer which I pray every day.

A MOMENT WITH THE LORD

You have called me, O Lord not so much because of me, but in spite of me; not so much to become a somebody, but to be a someone to You and to Your people. Keep me, O Lord, ever in Your love. Amen.

A MOMENT WITH THE WORD

"You did not choose me, I chose you.."

John 15:16

Correctional moment

Here is a story about hope.

At the Correctional Prison for Women, I met a seminarian who was three or four years from ordination. He was visiting his mother who was an inmate, but not just an inmate. His mother was a death-row inmate.

For a while I could not understand. "How can this be, Lord? In a few years this seminarian will be ordained and his mother is in death-row?"

"Can you not see Jerry? Something good can, and has come out, even from a seemingly bad and dark situation. Jerry, there is always hope," came the answer from the Lord.

A MOMENT WITH THE LORD

Lord, help me to see the good, the beautiful, the bright side, the hope and the reality of grace in every situation. Amen.

A MOMENT WITH THE WORD

"I solemnly assure you, unless a grain of wheat falls to the earth and dies, it remains just a grain of wheat. But if it dies, it produces much fruit."

John 12:24

Prophets for profits?

Someone once said that the business of preaching is to comfort the disturbed and to disturb the comfortable. When we find ourselves comforting those who are comfortable and disturbing those who are already disturbed, that means that we have ceased to become prophets. When we no longer do our role of challenging people to go beyond their comfort zones, when we no longer offer a vision to give hope and deeper meaning, then we have failed in our role to help people cross over their miseries and fears. And if we are not prophets, what are we but perpetuators of untruthfulness, partners and accomplices of injustices, agents of status quo, palliatives, and worse, plain court jesters and entertainers – prophets for profit.

A MOMENT WITH THE LORD

Lord, help me not to become a prophet just for profit. Amen.

A MOMENT WITH THE WORD

"I, the Lord, have called you and given you power to see that justice is done on earth."

Isaiah 42:6

Short cut entrance

I knew I was late for the Mass, so I rushed to the sacristy, hurriedly put on my vestments, and went straight to the sanctuary and kissed the altar. When I looked up to begin the Mass, the congregation was smiling because at the back of the church were the lectors, Eucharistic ministers, and servers who were all lined up, waiting for me for the procession, all scampering in haste toward the altar!

A MOMENT WITH THE LORD

Lord, help me not to forget my brothers and sisters on my journey to eternity. Amen.

A MOMENT WITH THE WORD

"Whoever does what my father in heaven wants is my brother, my sister, and my mother."

Matthew 12:50

Simple but beautiful life

My classmate, Fr. Charlie Cruz, SVD, from Orani, Bataan, passed away last 2005. He spent 19 years of his 60 years in this life in Togo, Africa as a missionary. Only God knows what sacrifices and hardships he went through in the service of his King, Christ the King. Also, only God knows the love he shared silently with so many people as a public school teacher before he entered the seminary, and as a formator and a confessor even while he was going through dialysis these past six years.

I am grateful to God for the simple but beautiful life he lived. After he died, I looked at his bare room. He left behind only a few clothes, some photo albums and some memorabilia here and there. Not much really, but he brings with him a bag full of love, lots of simple, pure, concrete love, to lay before the feet of Christ, the King.

A MOMENT WITH THE LORD

Lord, my king, help me to live a life full of love and meaning. Amen.

A MOMENT WITH THE WORD

"I was born with nothing and I will die with nothing."

Job 1:21

Spreading the light

The story is told about two coaches who happened to sit beside each other inside a church during Mass, obviously, praying for victory in the championship game that their opposing basketball teams were going to contest.

After Mass, one of the coaches lighted a candle before the image of St. Michael. The other coach, nervous that the lighted candle will give his rival coach's team an edge over his team, walked back to the church. Seeing that his rival coach was gone, guess what he did? He lit another candle?

No, he blew out the candle!

A MOMENT WITH THE LORD

Lord, help me not to be a candle blower but a candle lighter, so that I can spread your light. Amen.

A MOMENT WITH THE WORD

"Do not be yoked together with unbelievers. For what do righteousness and wickedness have in common? Or what fellowship can light have with darkness?."

1 Peter 2:11

What is a saint?

There is a story about a child who asked his father: "Dad, what is a saint?" The father was at a loss for words. Just then he saw the stained glass window of the church with images of saints and pointed to them. And the child said, "Oh, I know what saints are, Dad. They are the people in whom God's light shines through."

All of us can become modern-day "saints" if we let God's goodness, justice, truth and love shine through.

A MOMENT WITH THE LORD

Lord, may your love shine through me in spite of me. Amen.

A MOMENT WITH THE WORD

"I have given you a model to follow, so that as I have done for you, you should also do."

John 13:15

November

Our Lady of Guadalupe

Not Alone

Do you miss a loved one who had gone ahead? Below is a poem I read somewhere titled, "Alone, But Not Alone".

Alone yet never quite alone. I have an empty chair but sometimes in the silence, I imagine you are there. The good companion of the past, no longer here with me; and yet in some mysterious ways, you keep me company. Thought or spirit? Does it matter? Words are meaningless. I only know that in my times of greatest loneliness, I felt that you are somewhere near. Though nothing's seen or said, the bitter moment passes and my heart is comforted. I receive the strength I need, am rescued from despair; Maybe that's the way God works – the answer to a prayer. Though the pain is never lost and the future is unknown, I face the years that lie ahead, alone, yet not alone…

A MOMENT WITH THE LORD

Lord, because of you and the Resurrection, I am never alone, I will never be alone. Amen.

A MOMENT WITH THE WORD

Besides, they cannot die for they are like the angels. They, too, are sons and daughters of God because they are born of the Resurrection."

Luke 20:36

Reaching out to souls

How do I reach out to poor souls everyday? Whenever I read names in the obituary section of newspapers, I pray for them right away. Whenever I pass by a cemetery, or I happen to see a funeral procession, I would bless them. I recite the prayer, "Eternal rest grant unto them, O Lord, and let perpetual light shine upon them." And whenever I bless a dead person, I would ask its most powerful intercession for me and my special intentions.

That is how I reach out to souls in my simple way, every day.

A MOMENT WITH THE LORD

Eternal rest grant unto them, O Lord, and let perpetual light shine upon them. May they rest in peace. Amen.

A MOMENT WITH THE WORD

"I was born with nothing, and I will die with nothing."
Job 1:21

Dealing with death

The family was beyond consoling, and their only request to the mortician was to make their father look as if he was just sleeping (*parang natutulog lang...*). Sure enough when they viewed him in his coffin, he was in his pajamas, with his hands laid across his forehead!

And did you hear about the missionary who got the shock of his life when he came to bless the body of a village chief? The dead man lay in his coffin with his sunglasses on. Why? That had been his dying wish, the missionary found out later. The village chief had wanted to make sure that he could see Jesus when he faced Him in the dazzling beatific vision!

A MOMENT WITH THE LORD

Lord, help me always to look beyond the pain of death, and to see the joy of resurrection. Amen.

A MOMENT WITH THE WORD

"The God of all grace who called you to his eternal glory through Christ Jesus will Himself restore, confirm, strengthen and establish you."

1 Peter 5:10

Flowers, now

When was the last time you gave flowers to a loved one?

Why is it that we usually wait for a person to die before we give flowers? Nice, but *sayang*. It's really a pity to see all those beautiful flowers just go to waste, when in fact they would have been so welcomed and so appreciated by the person when he/she was still alive.

Little things mean a lot. Love them now while they are still alive. Do not postpone your loving. Do not wait for the grave...

A MOMENT WITH THE LORD

Lord, remind me that flowers, kind words and good deeds are more for the living, than for the dead. Amen.

A MOMENT WITH THE WORD

"Now is the time to wake out of sleep; for now our salvation is nearer than when we first believed."

Romans 13:11

Three P's

Married people need a lot of these three P's: Patience, Perseverance, and Prayers.

I know a couple whose marriage was on the rocks, and were about to separate. Nothing seemed to work anymore. It was as if something had died between them.

Through it all, the wife persevered in prayer and patience. Until one day, the husband walked up to her, admitted his faults, asked for forgiveness, and said: "For so long, I've been lost because I've focused on so many things. From now on, Mommy, the only focus of our marriage will be the salvation of our souls."

Husbands and wives, is the salvation of your souls a focus in your marriage, your family?

A MOMENT WITH THE LORD

Lord, no matter what happens, help me to be patient, persevering and prayerful. Amen.

A MOMENT WITH THE WORD

"He has not rejected my prayer; nor withheld his love from me."

Psalm 66:20b

The bishop's staff

There is a story about St. Patrick who carried a Bishop's staff as he went preaching Christianity all over Ireland. The staff had a sharp metal tip which lets it stand unaided on the ground.

In Munster, he was met by King Aengus who enthusiastically asked to be baptized. In the middle of the solemn ritual, St. Patrick accidentally drove the staff through the king's foot. The king, all red, uttered not a word of complaint.

Why? Because he thought the stabbing was just a normal part of the baptism..

A MOMENT WITH THE LORD

Lord, teach me not to complain, even when in pain. Amen.

A MOMENT WITH THE WORD

"Do everything without complaining or arguing."
Philippians 2:14

The flag of Korea

In November 1983, I received a letter from the SVD Superior General asking me to be a part of the founding team of the SVD in South Korea. It was a challenge which he told me to pray over for a month or so before I give my decision.

It was a month of being torn between "Go" and "No," for it was not easy to leave one's "familiar shores."

One night, I was with a family in Urdaneta, Pangasinan. The couple's 6-year-old child kept interrupting our conversation so I gave him a piece of paper to draw something. After some minutes, the child came up to me and showed me his drawing. I asked him what it was, he said, "Father, that's a flag, the flag of Korea!"

That night, I made my decision. The Lord has spoken through a child. It was a "Go."

A MOMENT WITH THE LORD

Lord, thank you for the many constant reminders of your presence and love through the years in my life. Amen.

A MOMENT WITH THE WORD

"Out of the mouths of babes and sucklings you have fashioned praise..."

Psalm 8:3

Be not afraid

I would like to share with you the lyrics of a song that has given me much courage and assurance all these years, especially when I was leaving for my mission assignment to South Korea way back in 1984.

"You shall cross the barren desert, but you shall not die of thirst. You shall wander far in safety, though you do not know the way. You shall speak your words to foreign men and they will understand. You shall see the face of God and live. Be not afraid. I go before you always. Come follow me, and I will give you rest. If you pass through raging waters in the sea, you shall not drown. If you walk amid the burning flames, you shall not be harmed. If you stand before the powers of hell and death is at your side, know that I am with you through it all... Be not afraid"

A MOMENT WITH THE LORD

Lord, in my journeys, and whenever I feel lost, be with me always. Amen.

A MOMENT WITH THE WORD

"Be not afraid, I am with you always."

Matthew 28:5,20

Overheard

I just overheard that the rule on priestly celibacy will soon be lifted!

Hooray!

However, I also heard that there are two conditions:

First, one must be at least 80 years old.

And second, one must have parental consent!

A MOMENT WITH THE LORD

Lord, when I give, help me to give joyfully and generously. Amen.

A MOMENT WITH THE WORD

"Serve the Lord with gladness, come before him with joyful song."

Psalm 100:2

Elusive dreams and schemes

The story is told about a man who searched for gold all his life. His one preoccupation and devotion was to accumulate more and more gold in life, sacrificing his health, his family, his friends, his values, and even his soul for precious, precious gold. When he died, St. Peter showed him the road to heaven. It was all paved with gold with the words: "That which you considered valuable and precious on earth is just asphalt here."

A MOMENT WITH THE LORD

Lord, help me not to live a life in pursuit of elusive dreams and schemes which will be useless and worthless in the end. Amen.

A MOMENT WITH THE WORD

"But seek first the kingdom of God and his righteousness, and all these things will be given besides."

Matthew 6:33

Hurry, worry, bury

Somebody once said that the lives of people these days can be summed up in three words: hurry, worry, bury. A lot of people are in a hurry and carry a lot of worry, and so, find themselves early in the cemetery. It's time for us to rediscover the 3R's in life: Relax, Reflect, Renew.

Statistics show that people's worries can be summed up thus: Things that never happened (40 percent); things that have happened and cannot be changed (30 percent); petty and needless worries (22 percent); legitimate worries which are beyond one's control (8 percent). So what are you worried about?

A MOMENT WITH THE LORD

Lord, remind me that when I worry and hurry, I go to the cemetery early. Amen.

A MOMENT WITH THE WORD

"Cast all your cares on Him because He cares for you."

1 Peter 5:7

Miracle?

The story is told about a Filipino who was questioned at the airport customs in Paris. "What's inside these huge boxes?" the inspector asked. "Only bottles of water from the Lourdes Grotto," said the Filipino. Upon sniffing the contents, the inspector said. "These are premium French wine!" Whereupon the Filipino exclaimed: "*Santissima!* Water turned to wine! Another miracle from Lourdes!"

A MOMENT WITH THE LORD

Lord, remind me that I may get away with it sometimes, but not all the time. Amen.

A MOMENT WITH THE WORD

"The measure with which you measure will be used to measure you."

Matthew 7:2

Who's talking?

Who's talking? They say that during courtship, the man talks and the woman listens. Once married, it is the wife who talks, and the husband listens. After some more years, both husband and wife talk, and the neighbors listen.

A MOMENT WITH THE LORD

Remind me Lord that true life is about pleasing You, and not so much myself, nor my neighbors. Amen.

A MOMENT WITH THE WORD

"For I always do what pleases him."

John 8:29

Bishop Manuel

Fr. Vicente Manuel, SVD was just an "ordinary" student in Christ the King Seminary by worldly standards. This shy *probinsiyano* from Calintaan, Occidental Mindoro had no chance to excel in a class that was studded with gifted and talented personalities. In fact, he literally had to go through the "narrow gate" to make it to the priesthood because of academics. But in 1983, this ordinary student became local ordinary of the Vicariate of San Jose Occidental Mindoro, the first bishop from their class.

Bishop Manuel, SVD, D.D. died last Aug. 18, 2007. He was then an auxiliary bishop in the Archdiocese of Cebu. But more than achievements, we remember the person. More than achievements, we remember moments. Because God's ways are not man's ways, whenever we look at people, we must not judge; neither must we just throw accolades. In the end, we leave everything in God's mercy and love.

A MOMENT WITH THE LORD

Lord, help me to live not just a successful life but a significant life. Amen.

A MOMENT WITH THE WORD

"The God of grace who called you to His eternal glory through Christ Jesus will Himself restore, confirm, strengthen, and establish you."

1 Peter 5:10

What is a father?

What is a father? A boy gave this beautiful response: "A father is a person who used to have money in his wallet but now only has pictures of his loved ones." I know of fathers who sacrifice so much, just so a son or a daughter will have a better life. As for those fathers who still have so much or too much money in their wallets, perhaps it's time for them to really examine their being a father: Do you need all that money? How did you make all that money? Is money all that important? Is money all that you'll leave behind?

A MOMENT WITH THE LORD

Lord, help us to be like you, our generous and loving Father. Amen.

A MOMENT WITH THE WORD

" I am the Lord, your God."

Hosea 13:4

Changes

Albert Einstein is said to have once said: "Men love women with the hope they will never change. Women love men with the hope they will change. Invariably they are both disappointed."

A MOMENT WITH THE LORD

Lord, thank you for loving me as I am, no matter what I am. Amen.

A MOMENT WITH THE WORD

"As clay in the potter's hand so are you in my hands."
Jeremiah 18:6

Going alone

Fr. Jun Castro, SVD, our missionary to Argentina, relates that one Christmas Eve, he was in a hurry to return to his main station after his barrio Mass to make a long distance call to his family back home. Many of the Mass goers wanted to hitch a ride, but he made excuses since he thought the weight of added passengers would slow him down. He regretted this decision later because the pick-up could not make it through the loose dirt road going uphill since it was too light. Soon the parishioners caught up with him, helped him out of the mess and all together they made it back. They chided him later saying, "You see Father, if you leave us, you'll never get to where you are going."

A MOMENT WITH THE LORD

Lord, remind me that our final destination is heaven, and that we need others to get there. Amen.

A MOMENT WITH THE WORD

" ...I will dwell in the house of the Lord for years to come ."

Psalm 23:6

Happiest day

For those who belittle the importance of the Eucharist, as they are so busy with their quest for wealth and achievements in this world, here is an anecdote from F.H. Dunkwater: Napoleon Bonaparte, who was known for his victorious conquests, was once asked by one of his generals what was the happiest day of his life. They thought he would mention his victory in Lombardy or Austerliz or the Bridge of Lodi. After a long pause, Napoleon replied, "The happiest day of my life? Ah -- that was the day of my first communion. I was near to God then."

A MOMENT WITH THE LORD

Lord, I want to be near You always. Amen.

A MOMENT WITH THE WORD

"You know when I sit and stand; you understand my thoughts from afar."

Psalm 139:2

Stand up for Christ!

There is an interesting story about a gunman who barged into a church one Sunday morning during the service and then called out: "Those of you here who are willing to die for Christ, step forward!"

Most of the faithful ran out in panic, but a few, too scared and stiff, stayed behind. Then the gunman said: "All right Father. The hypocrites are gone. Now you may start the Mass".

What if you were in that church? What if you were the priest in that church? Would you have run away?

A MOMENT WITH THE LORD

Lord, as you have always stood up for me, help me to stand up for you. Amen.

A MOMENT WITH THE WORD

"Don't ask me to leave you! Let me go with you. Wherever you go, I will go; Wherever you live, I will live..."

Ruth 1:16

Comfort zones

Going through the deserts of Egypt on our way to the Holy Land, this question cropped up in my mind: Why did God make deserts? What's the use of those vast tracts of arid land?

In the same way, we must have often asked God why He lets us pass through harsh deserts in this life? I really have no answers except that perhaps in the desert, one becomes more trusting and more in tune with God. Deprived of one's comfort zones, one can't help but reach out, and hold on to the One who disturbs and challenges comfort zones.

A MOMENT WITH THE LORD

Lord, remind me that true loving is a constant leaving of my comfort zones. Amen.

A MOMENT WITH THE WORD

"Love bears all things, believes all things, hopes all things, endures all things."

I Corinthians 13:7-8

Commitment

Somebody shared with me this story about children who were lined up in the cafeteria of a Catholic elementary school for lunch. At the head of the table was a large tray of apples with the note, written by a nun. "Take only one. God is watching." At the end of the table was a large pile of chocolate cookies. A child had a written note: "Take all you want. God is watching the apples."

A MOMENT WITH THE LORD

Lord, help me to go beyond legalisms and compromise, and to keep going the extra mile, and one more smile. Amen.

A MOMENT WITH THE WORD

"Be an example for the believers in your speech, your conduct, your love, faith and purity."

I Timothy 4:12

The electric fan

One way of understanding the mystery of the Trinity is to take a moment to look at an electric fan. There are three blades, but once the fan is switched on, we no longer see three blades, but one blade in motion. The motion within the Trinity is love, and we are called to be integrated in the love of the Father, Son, and the Holy Spirit.

A MOMENT WITH THE LORD

Lord, may I always be within the inner circle of Your love. Amen.

A MOMENT WITH THE WORD

"If anyone declares that Jesus is the Son of God, he lives in union with God and God lives in union with him."

I John 4:15

Do you have other 'kings'?

The story is told about a congressman who visited an old folks home. As part of his public campaign, he went around shaking hands with everyone. As the cameras clicked and rolled, he stopped for an old man at the corridor and asked him: "Lolo, do you know who I am?" The old man just stared at him and after some moments replied: "No, but if you'll ask one of the nurses, she'll tell you."

Jesus reminds us that our true identity is not about titles, positions, achievements or even our nationality. How do we look at ourselves? How do we look at other people?

We, who follow Christ the King must, in a world so full of hatred and materialism, continue to have good hearts and continue to be God's loving presence, in the here and now. That's what it means to stand for Christ the King. You, what do you stand for?

A MOMENT WITH THE LORD

Lord, You are my true King, and I have no other "kings" but You. Amen.

A MOMENT WITH THE WORD

"Seek first his kingship over you, his way of holiness and all these things will be given to you besides."

Matthew 6:33

Start spreading the news

There is a story about a barber who gave a free haircut to a German. The next day, he received a basket of frankfurters outside his door. After giving a Japanese also a free haircut, the barber found a bottle of "sake" outside his door. He gave a Filipino a free haircut and, the next day, what did the barber find? 10 more Filipinos who received and were sending text messages about a German giving a free haircut!

A MOMENT WITH THE LORD

Lord, use me to spread the good news wherever I am, wherever I go. Amen.

A MOMENT WITH THE WORD

"Do not deceive yourselves by just listening to his word; instead, put it into practice".

James 1:22

Our Mother

There is a story I heard about a nervous sinner who was welcomed by Jesus in heaven.

"You know me, Lord?" asked the sinner.

"Yes, I know you. My mother told me all about you." Jesus replied.

"But I don't even know your Mother," protested the sinner.

"That's all right. Your mother never ceased telling things about you to my Mother." Jesus said with a smile.

A MOMENT WITH THE LORD

Lord, thank you, for my mother and our Mother. Amen.

A MOMENT WITH THE WORD

"Then he said to the disciple, 'She is your mother.'"

John 19:27

Letting go and holding on

When was the last time you flew a kite?

When was the last time you went fishing?

Flying a kite and fishing remind us of our young and carefree days. They also remind us of basic lessons in life, namely:

We need to be connected.

We cannot be on the loose.

We need to learn when to hold on and when to let go.

We need to come home in the end.

A MOMENT WITH THE LORD

Lord, help me to stay connected with you so that I can find my way back home. Amen.

A MOMENT WITH THE WORD

"Remain in me as I in you... I am the vine , you are the branches."

John 15: 4-5

Like father, like son

The story is told about a nurse who, upon coming out of the delivery room, motioned to an expectant father and declared, "You have a son!" Another man jumped up and cried, "Say, what's the big idea? I was here before he was!"

Jesus teaches us that we have a generous and giving Father. In contrast, we His children are selfish, proud and stingy toward each other. It's time for us to reflect once more on the saying "Like father, like son / daughter."

A MOMENT WITH THE LORD

Lord, help me to reflect your image as I live my life. Amen.

A MOMENT WITH THE WORD

"I urge you, imitate me."

1 Corinthians 4: 16

Lion and the mouse

The story is told about a proud lion who visited a tiny mouse. "Hey mouse, I'm getting married. What's the best advice you can give?" the lion asked.

"Just remember this my friend, I too was a lion before I got married," said the mouse.

A MOMENT WITH THE LORD

Lord, remove my illusion that I am bigger than what I really am. Amen.

A MOMENT WITH THE WORD

"God resists the proud but bestows His favor on the lowly."

James 4:6

Oberammergau

I had the privilege of seeing the "Passionspiele," the passion play at Oberammergau in Germany. The whole town takes part in the play, which is staged every ten years, out of gratitude for having been spared from the plague of 1633. The play runs from May to October, five days a week. About 5,000 people watch every play day.

The play is really very impressive and very moving. However, I had one disappointment. After the play I thought that people would fill up the church to hear Mass and to be with the same Jesus so beautifully portrayed in the play. But there were just a handful of us. I guess people were there just for the play, and not to pray.

A MOMENT WITH THE LORD

Lord, help me to appreciate Your presence in my life, in people, and especially in the Eucharist. Amen.

A MOMENT WITH THE WORD

" Do not deceive yourselves by just listening to his word; instead, put it into practice."

James 1:22

Rationalizations

The story is told about a man who boasted that he had 16 wives. When asked why he felt justified for having done so, his answer is that he married, 4 better, 4 worse, 4 richer, 4 poorer! To complete his rationalization, he further boasted that he could divorce eight of these wives. His reason? "Till d 8th do us part."

A MOMENT WITH THE LORD

Lord, remind me that relationships is not about commodity but fidelity. Amen.

A MOMENT WITH THE WORD

"Let not kindness and fidelity leave you."

Proverbs 3:3

**Immaculate
Conception**

Religious

The story is told about an airplane that was going through turbulent weather. The passengers were all quiet and scared. Some were screaming and praying, except one boisterous man who was joking and enticing every one to just relax and drink. The woman beside him scolded him and said: "We are going to crash! Why don't you do...don't you do something religious or godly for once in your life?" Upon hearing this, the man stood up and started a collection down the aisle.

A MOMENT WITH THE LORD

Lord, help me not to make you just an appendage or an after-thought in my life. Amen.

A MOMENT WITH THE WORD

"Serve the Lord with gladness, come before him with joyful song."

Psalm 100: 2

Slow down

Someone said that if you treat a cold, it lasts for seven days. If you don't treat it, it lasts for one week! So, when cold comes, all we really need is rest, lots of liquid and lots of sleep.

Slow down.

A MOMENT WITH THE LORD

Lord, help me to slow down and be silent, so that I can listen to you. Amen.

A MOMENT WITH THE WORD

"By the seventh day the work God had done was completed, and he rested on the seventh day from all the work he had done."

Genesis 2:2

Smile

For those of you who seldom or have forgotten to smile, listen to this text message:

Smile is the best lighting system of the face, the best cooling system of the head, and the best warming system of the heart."

When was the last time you smiled?

Smile *naman dyan,o!*

A MOMENT WITH THE LORD

Lord, you are a God who always smiles at me with love. Help me always to show that. Amen.

A MOMENT WITH THE WORD

"Add a smiling face to all your gifts."

Ecclesiastes 35:8

Where to?

The story is told about a priest giving the last rites to a dying man. He kept telling him: "Curse Satan. Renounce him now!" The dying man opened his eyes and said: "No way, Father. I'm not offending anyone until I know where I'm going."

Do you know where you're going?

A MOMENT WITH THE LORD

Lord, remind me that from you I came, to you I will go back. Amen.

A MOMENT WITH THE WORD

"Prepare to meet your God."

Amos 4:12

Walk the talk

I would like to share with you a concrete example of "walking the talk." In the Mission House where I am staying, we have a common house phone, and whenever it rings, especially at an "unholy hour," I am often tempted to let it go on ringing, hoping that some "less busy" priest would pick it up, because picking it up would mean either going to a sick call, hearing a confession or climbing a flight of stairs looking for someone needed on the phone. I resolved this with this thought: It is God who is calling; all of us are busy loving; no such thing as "unholy hour" in the business of loving.

A MOMENT WITH THE LORD

Lord, help me to walk my talk. Amen.

A MOMENT WITH THE WORD

"Let as not grow weary while doing good, for in due season we shall reap if we do not lose heart."

Galatians 4:6

The little ones

In my radio program, "Hello Father" at Radio Veritas, I get lots of calls from children. How touching to hear these little angels who are so innocent and honest.

Once, a 6-year-old boy asked live on air, for prayers for his father to come back to their family so that his mother would stop crying. Another time, a little girl asked for prayers for her father to stop beating up her mother. These and many more heartbreaking stories should remind us adults how much we can affect the little ones. Big people have big responsibilities. To whom much is given, much is also required! What sort of examples are we giving and what values are we leaving unto the little ones?

A MOMENT WITH THE LORD

Lord, remind me that I was once a child, needing all the help and love in this life. Amen.

A MOMENT WITH THE WORD

"Grandchildren are the crown of old men, and the glory of children is their parentage."

Proverbs 17:6

Aquarium

Recently, I revived a "love of my life" when I was a little boy: having an aquarium. It was a boyhood fascination. As I grew up, I became busier and forgot all about it. But the heart never, never really forgets. So when I shared with my friends my desire to put a little aquarium in my room, one said he was giving me an old aquarium he was no longer using. One morning, I set it up, filled it with water and put two gold fishes, two black mollies and two swordtails. It really brought back many memories. I was all smiles when I left my room to go to my appointments for the day.

When I came back at night, the floor in my room was flooded, the aquarium was empty, and the fish were all dead. Why? There was a leak in the aquarium. Everything I set up was new and alive, except the aquarium which was old and defective.

A MOMENT WITH THE LORD

Lord, remind me that everything that I have set up or acquired can be gone in the wink of an eye. Amen.

A MOMENT WITH THE WORD

"Do not consider yourself wise, fear God, and turn away from evil."

Proverbs 3:7

They say little...

I would like to confess now that some of the best years of my life were spent in the arms of a woman.... my mother!

These days, I often find myself looking with a smile and so much love at Mama, now 86 years old, this woman who has loved me so much all these 54 years of my earthly existence. She has really loved much, and she did it all with so much humility and simplicity. She went through a lot of difficulties raising all five of us. I thank God that I have many memories of love from her, and the most unforgettable is waking up at night, seeing her covering us with a blanket, making sure that we her children were all right. Yes, they say little who love much...

A MOMENT WITH THE LORD

Lord, thank You for the love and gentleness which I have received and learned from Mama. Amen.

A MOMENT WITH THE WORD

"We were gentle among you, just as a nursing mother cherishes her own children."

I Thessalonians 2:7

Abra

In Abra where I served as a missionary for a year, I learned how to bring a jeep across a river. If one had a sacristan, he could wade ahead and find the shallow part of the river. If one is alone, all it took was to throw a stone into the water, and just by the sound, know if the water ahead was shallow or deep.

A MOMENT WITH THE LORD

Lord, I hope my love for you is deep enough. Amen.

A MOMENT WITH THE WORD

"Blessed is the man who find wisdom, the man who gains understanding, for he is more profitable than silver and yields better returns than gold."

Proverbs 3:13-14

Dream on

The story is told about an interviewer who asked; "What would you do if one morning you woke up and found beside you $1 million?"

The American responded that he would go on a world tour. The Japanese said he would put up a luxury hotel. The Chinese said he'd put it all in stocks. The Filipino said he'd sleep again, so that when he woke up he'd have another million!

A MOMENT WITH THE LORD

Lord, help me not just to dream, but work to make my dreams come true. Amen.

A MOMENT WITH THE WORD

"A man's heart plans his way, but the Lord directs his steps."

Proverbs 16:9

Car wash

Washing a car is pretty much the same as washing your heart.

First, the car must be still so that it can be washed. The heart too must be silent, so that it can listen (notice the same letter involved in the words "silent" and "listen"?). God cannot speak to a noisy heart.

Second, the car, like the heart must be obedient and submissive.

God cannot speak to a heart that denies, rationalizes or postpones.

Third, the car, like the heart must be open so that all the deepest corners and chambers can be reached and cleaned. In the same way, God cannot clean and heal a heart that is closed tight.

A MOMENT WITH THE LORD

Lord, help me to be silent, so that I can really listen. Amen.

A MOMENT WITH THE WORD

"Search me, O God and know my heart."

Psalm 139:23

Hold on

The story is told about a mother who told her little girl: "No matter what happens, hold on to my skirt so that you won't get lost in the mall." "Yes, Mommy," was the little girl's reply.

There were so many people doing their last-minute Christmas shopping, and true enough, the little girl held on, and held on tight.

Two hours later, there was an announcement: "Calling on the parent or guardian of a lost little girl wearing a blue dress and tenaciously holding on to a red skirt."

A MOMENT WITH THE LORD

Lord, help me to hold on to you no matter what, no matter where. Amen.

A MOMENT WITH THE WORD

"I am the vine. You are the branches. Remain in my love."

John 15:5,9

Christmas along the *riles*

A Christmas moment happened when I presided over a street dawn Mass in Sampaloc's "home along the riles." As I started the Mass, I noticed that I was audible but not visible to the people positioned at the sides of the street because the altar was inside the garage of an apartment. So I stopped and asked the lay ministers to bring out the altar right into the street where I could be seen and heard by all.

Maybe that's what Christmas is all about – God wanting to be seen, heard and touched by ordinary people – so he left his comfortable niche and became one of us, and dwelt among us.

This Christmas get out of your comfort zones and reach out to God in gratitude, to your own family, and to people around you who need your compassion.

A MOMENT WITH THE LORD

Lord, teach me to be compassionate and make every day a Christmas day. Amen.

A MOMENT WITH THE WORD

"Jesus did not count equality with God a thing to be grasped. He emptied himself, taking the form of a servant, being born in the likeness of men..."

Philippians 2:6-7

'Mary' Christmas

"Mary Christmas, *Pader!*" I smiled when I heard this greeting from the driver who brought me back from a dawn Mass. In fact, I wanted to correct his pronunciation, but realized at the very moment the real meaning of Christmas...the first Christmas was Mama Mary's Christmas! It was simple, peaceful, joyful, and full of hope. It was indeed a "Mary Christmas."

"Mary Christmas to you, too," I answered as I thanked the driver. The incident reminded me that more than a merry Christmas, may we experience a "Mary Christmas" and not be a *pader* (wall) especially at Christmas.

A MOMENT WITH THE LORD

Lord, help me to make all my Christmases a "Mary Christmas," full of simplicity, peace, joy, and hope. Amen.

A MOMENT WITH THE WORD

"She wrapped Him in swaddling clothes..."

Luke 2:7

Blessed silence

Did you know that the Trappist Monks used to observe perpetual silence in their monasteries? They were not allowed to talk to each other. Only to God, in prayers. But on Christmas day, they were allowed to share.

I heard the story of two monks, who were conversing with each other, then the bell rang signalling the end of their sharing. After one year, on Christmas day, the two monks met again, and one of them started, "Ah, as I was saying last year…"

A MOMENT WITH THE LORD

Lord, help me to offer everything with joy and gratitude. Amen.

A MOMENT WITH THE WORD

"Do all things without complaining."

Philippians 2:14

A child at Christmas

I was on my sixth day of Christmas *misa de gallo* (early morning novena Masses), and fatigue and lack of sleep were taking their toll on me. At Communion, I felt dizzy, so I had to sit down. I didn't know what prompted me to do it, but I asked a little boy of seven to hold the ciborium in front, and asked the congregation to come and receive Holy Communion. As I sat there looking at this little boy smiling so happily at all who came forward, it dawned on me that this was what Christmas was all about! A child was born, given to us, offering Himself to each one of us!

A MOMENT WITH THE LORD

Lord, thank you for offering Your very self to me. Forgive me for the times I rejected, disregarded, belittled or even snubbed Your loving offer to me. Amen.

A MOMENT WITH THE WORD

"God so loved the world He gave his only Son."

John 3:16

A Golden Acres moment

It all happened very fast. A group of volunteers and I were at a Christmas party for the old and the abandoned. Everybody was having a good time, particularly an old woman who was dancing like a child. Then she collapsed, and in no time at all she was dead.

I blessed her lifeless body under a white sheet in the tiny room she had lived in for 15 years. There was nothing there. It was bare, except for her rubber slippers, a plastic pail and *tabo*, and a plastic bag with all her worldly possessions. Even her funeral would be simple. No relatives, no flowers, no obituary. Only one lighted candle kept vigil when she said goodbye to the world.

A MOMENT WITH THE LORD

Lord, remind me that I take nothing with me when I bid this world goodbye, except the love I shared in this life and the promise of eternal life. Amen.

A MOMENT WITH THE WORD

"Naked I came forth from my mother's womb, and naked shall I go back again."

Job 1:21

Remembering Papa

My father was a giver.

He gave twenty three years of his life to honest, dedicated public service. He could have enriched himself as the Collector of Customs in the Port of Manila, but he chose a good name and a clean conscience above material wealth.

He was generous to a fault. He died a poor man. Three days before his interment we still had no place to bury him. Why? Because he had given away his memorial plan to some needy relative.

He died a poor man, but for me he was rich with God and with people. To this very day, I meet people who knew him and would tell me: "I knew your father. He was a good man."

A MOMENT WITH THE LORD

Lord, between being rich and being good, help me to choose being good. Amen.

A MOMENT WITH THE WORD

"It is better to be poor and honest than to be a fool and dishonest."

Proverbs 19:1

Christmas with the MC's

For many of us, Christmas especially Christmas eve, is a time to feel good, to feel cozy and nice. Christmas is the time of the year when there is an abundance of food, gifts, good cheer and merrymaking. But for many more people, Christmas is just an ordinary day, nothing to feel cozy or nice about. At Christmas, more than any other time of the year, they know and become aware that they don't have much...nothing at all.

The realization dawned on me one Christmas morning at a Mass for the Missionaries of Charity in Tondo, Manila. Amid the heat, stench, sickness, and poverty, there was the reality of the Incarnation in our present day and time.

A MOMENT WITH THE LORD

Lord, help me not just to feel Christmas. Help me to make Christmas a reality, especially for the poor and the needy. Amen.

A MOMENT WITH THE WORD

"Jesus did not count equality with God a thing to be grasped. He emptied Himself, taking the form of a servant, being born in the likeness of men."

Philippians 2:6-7

A sidewalk Christmas

I stopped to say hello to my friends Sonny and Jean and others who were gathered in a dimly lit sidewalk one late December evening, keeping vigil for the woman who was in labor in a little hut nearby.

The night was quiet. The stars were shining brightly. And then, the faint cry of a newborn baby! We looked at each other with a smile. Then, we went up to gather together in thanksgiving prayer, and to bless mother and child.

The room was so bare, austere, and simple. It was a Christmas night I will long remember.

A MOMENT WITH THE LORD

Lord, remind me that you came to this world poor, and you left this world poor. Amen.

A MOMENT WITH THE WORD

"There was no room for them in the inn."

Luke 2:7

Making Christmas happen

I still become teary eyed whenever I remember the poverty and deprivations I experienced as a little boy, especially at Christmas. But my tears were tears of joy and gratitude for Papa and Mama who tried to make Christmas happen where it mattered most – in the heart of a child.

One Christmas morning, I remember how I and my brothers and sisters excitedly opened the big boxes all wrapped up under the Christmas tree. Lo and behold, inside the boxes were *suman, bibingka, binongey,* and other native cakes. Papa and Mama had no toys to wrap for us, but they still gave, and made Christmas happen for us.

A MOMENT WITH THE LORD

Lord, remind me not to be burdened by obstacles and deprivations. Help me to see not the stumbling blocks but the stepping stones as I go on. Amen.

A MOMENT WITH THE WORD

"For when I, too, was a little boy and my mother fondly looked at me as special; my father taught me and said to me: treasure my words in your hearts, listen to my directions and you will live."

Proverbs 4:3-4

Crib moment

It was my first Christmas as a Campus Minister in Divine Word College of Urdaneta, Pangasinan, and I wanted to make the students realize the meaning of Christmas.

One morning, the students saw a "belen," the Nativity scene, right beside the chapel, and their attention was caught by the empty crib of Baby Jesus. It was not at all a pleasant sight. In fact, many were aghast, even angry, because the crib was filled with broken glass, nails, thumbtacks and trash.

I posted a simple message in the crib which read: "Is your heart like this when He comes?" ("*Ganito ba ang iyong puso sa Kanyang pagdating?*")

A MOMENT WITH THE LORD

Lord, remove the dirt and the thorns in my heart, so that You and my brothers and sisters will always find a happy welcome there. Amen.

A MOMENT WITH THE WORD

"A clean heart create for me, O God, and a steadfast spirit renew within me."

Psalm 51:12

Presence, not presents

The story is told about three brothers, who after years of hard work and leading busy lives, wanted to make their 83-year-old mother happy especially on Christmas Day. To make up for the years when they neglected her and took her for granted, the eldest gifted her with a big house. The second son surprised her with a limousine, and the youngest gifted her with an expensive parrot that can recite the whole Bible.

After the holidays, they received a thank you note from their mother. To the first one she wrote: "Thank you for the house, but it is so big I can't clean it myself." To the second one, she wrote: "The car is so beautiful, but I never use it because I have nowhere to go." To the youngest, she scribbled: "You gave me the best gift. The chicken was delicious!"

A MOMENT WITH THE LORD

Lord, as we prepare for Christmas, let us be reminded again that our presents are a poor substitute for our presence. Amen.

A MOMENT WITH THE WORD

"Love one another with mutual affection; anticipate one another in showing honor."

Romans 12:10

What if...

Think about it: There were people who were with us last Christmas and are no longer with us this Christmas... And there are people who are with us this Christmas who may not be anymore with us next Christmas... So, why don't you make this Christmas the best Christmas ever yet.

What if it was his/her last Christmas...

What if it was your last Christmas...

Morbid? Maybe, but the message is clear: Do not postpone your reconciliation with your God and your expressions of love for others, especially your loved ones, this Christmas.

A MOMENT WITH THE LORD

Lord, help me to love now. Help me not to postpone my loving and my coming back to you. Amen.

A MOMENT WITH THE WORD

"Stay awake, then, for you do not know on what day your Lord will come."

Matthew 24:42

Game *ka na ba?*

What if something did not go right on the first Christmas? What if Mary and Joseph did not cooperate with God's plan? What if, for example, Mary refused to become the Mother of God?

And what if Joseph, being a righteous man, refused to be a part of the shameful situation? After all, it was a case of teenage pregnancy and the father was unknown! Or worse, what if the two decided to abort the Baby to avoid the hassles and inconveniences of raising a child, and just went on with their normal lives?

Anything could have happened. In fact, Joseph thought of divorcing Mary quite early on. God's eternal plan rested on the "yes" of these two ordinary mortals. The whole company of angels must have paused and prayed hard as the two pondered their decision. It could have gone either way: that of becoming the "weakest link" or Game *na!*"

For Mary and Joseph, it was "Game *na!*"

A MOMENT WITH THE LORD

Lord, help me celebrate Christmas with no ifs and live a lifetime with no buts. Amen.

A MOMENT WITH THE WORD

"Mary said: 'I am the servant of the Lord. Let it be done to me as you say.'"

Luke 1:38

A good family

Take a moment to look at your family.

What is a good family?
These are the three marks of a good family:

- close to God
- close to one another
- close to people

Some families are close to God, but they are not close to one another. Some families are close to God and to one another, but they are not close to people. And it could happen that some families are close to the people and to one another, but they are not close to God.

So, how is your family?

A MOMENT WITH THE LORD

Lord, I ask You to bless my family. Help me to make my family close to You, close to one another, and close to the people. Amen.

A MOMENT WITH THE WORD

"If we walk in the light as he is in the light, we have fellowship with one another."

John 1:17

Duplicate

The story is told about a farmer's wife who gave birth to twin girls. The first one they named "Kate". The second one, for want of a better name, they named "Duplikate."

A MOMENT WITH THE LORD

Lord, remind me that in your eyes there are no copycats or duplicates. Amen.

A MOMENT WITH THE WORD

" Because you are precious to me and honored, I love you."

Isaiah 43:3

Enough for me to know

Allow me to share with you the lyrics of a song I made and which I sing especially when I experience trials and pains:

Lord, you can make it tough, but don't make it impossible; You can make it hard, but Lord, please make it bearable; Lord, hear my prayer and wash away all my fears; In all these pains I suffer, You love me and you're near; and Lord, your love is all that matters!

"My child, be brave. Be not afraid. I love you. I am near."

Lord, you can make it tough; And you can make it hard. Enough for me to know I am loved!

A MOMENT WITH THE LORD

Lord, thank you for being with me, always. Amen.

A MOMENT WITH THE WORD

"... but Christ is all that matters."

Colossians 3:11

See you in heaven

Remember a loved one who had gone ahead. If only he or she could speak to you now, there are three things he or she would like to tell you:

"I'm ok. I am now in this kingdom where there are no more tears, no more pain, no more problems, no more sorrow, no more goodbyes. I am with my Creator. I am at peace."

"Thank you for all the love you have given to me when I was still alive and even now."

"See you in heaven! Live your life in such a way that you, too, will go to heaven at the end of your life. Here I want you, till we meet again."

May the death of a loved one bear fruit in each and every one of us who are left behind.

A MOMENT WITH THE LORD

Lord, help me to live my life in such a way that when I die, I too, will go to heaven. Amen.

A MOMENT WITH THE WORD

"In all your actions remember your last days and you will never sin."

Sirach 7:36

No burdens

Someone shared the following angel thought: "Do you know why angels can fly? It is not because they have wings: it is because they carry no burdens…."

A MOMENT WITH THE LORD

Lord, help me to learn how to surrender my burdens to You. Amen .

A MOMENT WITH THE WORD

"I will carry you!… Even I will carry and deliver you."
Isaiah 46:4

Treasure every moment

Think about it: "To realize the value of one year, ask a student who failed and has to repeat one school year; to realize the value of one month, ask a mother who gave birth to a premature baby; to realize the value of one week, ask the editor of a weekly newspaper; to realize the value of one hour, ask lovers who are waiting to meet each other; to realize the value of one minute, ask a person who missed the train; to realize the value of one second, ask a person who just avoided an accident."

A MOMENT WITH THE LORD

Lord, help me to treasure every moment, and help me to live each day to the fullest. Amen.

A MOMENT WITH THE WORD

"Teach us to number our days aright, that we may gain wisdom of heart."

Psalm 90:12

A word of thanks

This book would not have been made possible without the untiring support of the *Moments Foundation* which has been a great help in my media apostolate. My sincerest gratitude to the following members: Ella Sanchez, Lalin Basilio, Nita Trofeo, Vivian Eleazar, Marilou Estrada, Fritzy Lopez, Lydia Apuyan-Tagle, Rebbie Garcia, Jeffrey Campos, Emmanuel Magbag, Manny Sta. Cruz, Adrian Panganiban, Lilibeth Francisco, Dra. Nemy Platon, and Bayani Ting.

Special thanks also to Chito & Galoy Marfil, Mea Marfil, Ronnie Nazarea, Oscar & Mila Balaoing, Jonathan Atos, Maita Martinez, Nida Esteras, Letty dela Merced, and Angie Gabriel for their creative work and dedication.

Most especially, thank you, dear readers, for believing in *Moments...*

One with you.
Mama Mary loves you!

SVD Mission Office, P.O. Box 1375, Manila Philippines
Tel.: (63-2) 721-7457 Telefax: (63-2) 727-1160
E-mail: *jorbos@manila-online.net*